The Landscape of Nightmare

THE LANDSCAPE OF NIGHTMARE:

Studies in the Contemporary American Novel

By *JONATHAN BAUMBACH*

NEW YORK UNIVERSITY PRESS

813.509
B347l

Fourth printing 1970

ISBN-0-8147-0031-4 Cloth Edition
ISBN-0-8147-0032-2 Paper Edition

© 1965 BY NEW YORK UNIVERSITY
LIBRARY OF CONGRESS CATALOG CARD NUMBER: 65-11761
MANUFACTURED IN THE UNITED STATES OF AMERICA
DISTRIBUTED BY NEW YORK UNIVERSITY PRESS

ACKNOWLEDGMENTS

Dangling Man and *The Victim* by Saul Bellow are quoted by permission of Vanguard Press, Inc. and Weidenfeld & Nicolson, Ltd.

Invisible Man by Ralph Ellison is quoted by permission of Random House, Inc., Penguin Books, Ltd., and Lawrence Pollinger, Ltd.

The Natural, The Assistant, and *A New Life* by Bernard Malamud are quoted by permission of Farrar, Straus & Company, Inc. and Eyre & Spottiswoode, Ltd.

Ceremony in Lone Tree by Wright Morris (Copyright © 1959 by Wright Morris) is quoted by permission of Atheneum Publishers and Weidenfeld & Nicolson, Ltd.

Wise Blood by Flannery O'Connor is quoted by permission of Farrar, Straus & Company, Inc. and A. M. Heath & Company, Ltd.

Lie Down in Darkness and *Set This House on Fire* by William Styron are quoted by permission of The Bobbs-Merrill Company, Inc., Random House, Inc., and Hamish Hamilton, Ltd.

The Human Season, The Pawnbroker, and *The Tenants of Moonbloom* by Edward Lewis Wallant are quoted by permission of Harcourt, Brace & World, Inc., Victor Gollancz, Ltd., and Hughes Massie, Ltd.

v

All the King's Men by Robert Penn Warren is quoted by permission of Harcourt, Brace & World, Inc. and Eyre & Spottiswoode, Ltd.

Portions of this book appeared first in somewhat different form in *Critique, The Georgia Review, The Kenyon Review, Modern Language Quarterly, The Saturday Review, The South Atlantic Quarterly.*

for my son David
who is learning to read

TO LIVE in this world, to live consciously in this world in which madness daily passes for sanity is a kind of madness in itself. Yet where else can we go? We are born into this nightmare and we do our best (with a sense of initiative, duty, and honor —with no sense at all) to make the worst of it. And for all our massive efforts at self-extinction we continue to survive—a cosmic joke. Our novelists, unlike our journalists who (practical people) believe in the world they see, have tried to make sense —to make art—out of what it's like to live in this nightmare. The present book is, through the limitation of my own vision, a record of the vision of nine post-Second-World-War American novelists. These novels are discussed here not, however, as nightmare news reports of our culture, but as works of the imagination, as works that preserve the possibility of consciousness. As works of art.

Columbus, Ohio
August 1964

—JONATHAN BAUMBACH

CONTENTS

"But I am not guilty," said K.; "it's a mistake. And, if it comes to that, how can any man be called guilty? We are all simply men here, one is as much as the other."

"That is true," said the priest, "but that's how all guilty men talk."

—Franz Kafka

Interviewer: Modern art has that sense of danger?
Mailer: It has a sense of doom.

—*The Presidential Papers*

It is the *nature* of the future, not its extinction, that produces in the artist such foreboding, the prescient chill of heart of a world without consciousness.

—Wright Morris

The Landscape of Nightmare

1 · Introduction

> The only way to escape misrepresentation is never to commit oneself to any critical judgment that makes an impact—that is never to *say* anything.
> —*The Great Tradition*, F. R. Leavis

1

IT HAS become commonplace in recent years to complain that the novel as form is either dead or deathly ill, that we are living in a time relatively uncongenial to the making of literature, an age of criticism—a myth, incidentally, propagated by critics who have grown tired of reading. For all the banal horrors of our culture, the gradual deadening of our nerve of outrage, there has probably been in the past two decades as great a concentration of good American novels as in that mythic period of exile and return following the First World War. If we have at the moment more good novelists, we have also, perhaps—our proximity makes it difficult to know—fewer great ones. With the potential exception of Saul Bellow, no one of the current generation seems a titan of the stature of Faulkner or Hemingway. Nevertheless, the achievement in sum of such post-Second-World-War novelists as Robert Penn Warren, Saul Bellow, James Baldwin, Edward Lewis Wallant, William Burroughs, J. D. Salinger, Norman Mailer, Vance Bourjaily, Flannery O'Connor, Bernard Malamud, Wright Morris, Nelson Algren, James Jones, Ralph Ellison, William Styron, Carson McCullers, Truman Capote, John Updike, Herbert Gold, John Hawkes, John Barth, Philip Roth and others is considerable enough to allay all rumors of the novel's untimely death. If we are bent on attending a funeral, we will have to find the comfort of a corpse elsewhere.

If, as our social critics tell us, the American cultural climate is arid and degenerative, how is it possible that the novel is flourishing? If, as Dwight McDonald points out, the mass quasi-literacy of mid-cult has by and large adulterated our serious arts, why then the regeneration of the serious novel? [1] I can hope only to suggest some possible answers, all of which may be incidental, and none of which explains the genetic causes of literary genius. We are, despite present intimations of ulcerous middle age, a young culture just reaching maturity. Though we have out of the proprietary spirit of Puritan vanity hoarded our innocence longer than any other culture, in recent years we have, for better or worse, lost it more thoroughly. In a symbolic though perhaps not actual sense, the day we let loose the bomb on Hiroshima marked the point of no return of, at the very least, the myth of our innocence. I mention the bomb, though it is at once too easy and too complex an explanation, because no matter how we evade it, through disbelief or resignation, it is part of our consciousness.

For a conspiracy of reasons, not the least of which are the Doomsday alternatives of nuclear extinction or dehumanized survival, the post-Second-World-War American novel is not so much concerned with social defeats and victories as with adamic falls and quixotic redemptions. That is, rather than concentrating on the society in which man eats, drinks, loves, and gets promoted, the novel of the fifties explores by and large the shadow landscape of the self, often in the disguise of a dimly recognizable "real" world—a mythic world more consequential than the one it pretends to represent, more believable and horrible, more possible to survive in. Discussing the limitation of John Steinbeck's vision, R. W. B. Lewis in *The Picaresque Saint* suggests the preoccupation of the most serious contemporary fiction:

There is too indistinct an awareness in Steinbeck that the conventional terms of battle are no longer valid; that the guilt is everywhere and on all sides and in all of us, and the urge to expiate guilt as well; that the problem of the problematical novel is nothing less than the nature of man.

1 "Masscult and Midcult" in *Partisan Review*, Vol. XXVII, No. 4 (Fall, 1960). "Midcult has it both ways: it pretends to respect the standards of High Culture while in fact it waters them down and vulgarizes them."

The nature of man. That's where we all came in. And how different his nature seems (and how similar) and how terrifying from novel to novel. The hero of the contemporary American novel is often a sensitized outsider, what the sociologists call a marginal man, a kind of seismographic *schlemiel,* who, experiencing in magnification the sin and guilt of his contemporaries, sacrifices himself quixotically for their redemption or performs an exemplary spiritual passage for his own salvation (or fails painfully in the attempt). Though generally not religious in a traditional sense, a large number of our recent novels are almost paradigms of the existential possibilities (and impossibilities) of sainthood.

The main tradition of the American novel, if such a free-wheeling form can be said to have one, is founded on that ambiguity that Richard Chase calls the romance. In *The American Novel and Its Traditions,* Chase defines the term attributively as:

an assumed freedom from the ordinary novelistic requirements of verisimilitude, development, and continuity; a tendency toward melodrama and idyl; a more or less formal abstractness, and, on the other hand, a tendency to plunge into the underside of consciousness; a willingness to abandon moral questions or to ignore the spectacle of man in society or to consider these things only indirectly and abstractly.

I quote Chase's definition here because, with certain modifications, it also describes some of the concerns of our best recent fiction. One thinks immediately of *The Natural; Henderson the Rain King; Other Voices, Other Rooms; Barbary Shore; Wise Blood; Set this House on Fire; The Fable;* and *Invisible Man* as novels having more or less the qualities ascribed to the romance tradition. Since 1945 the serious American novel has moved away from naturalism and the social scene to explore the underside of consciousness (the "heart of darkness"), delineating in its various ways the burden and ambivalence of personal responsibility in a world which accommodates evil—that nightmare landscape we all inhabit. If there is a great tradition in the American novel, it cannot exclude our one undoubted prose masterpiece *Moby Dick* nor, for that matter, *The Scarlet Letter, The Confidence Man,* and *Huckleberry Finn,* all of

which are in the "classic sense" unnovelistic. Yet if they are unnovelistic in the English tradition, they are nevertheless in what
is apparently the main tradition of American prose fiction.
What makes the novel so engaging a form is that it has no
classic prototypes—that it is a genre of originals, of, in the
original sense of the word, novels.[2]

The serious novel of manners in America has become a rare
if not extinct breed. The fiction of John O'Hara, conceived of
the immaculate union of Fitzgerald and Hemingway, represents
an aspect of its desolation. Concerned with the eating, drinking,
and sleeping habits of the American middle class, O'Hara's
novels, with the exception of *Appointment in Samarra*, proliferate meaningless experience under the apparent assumption
that massive documentation is meaning, that the sheer weight
of the whole will transcend the meaninglessness of each of its
parts. There is always too much amassed, but never, of course,
enough. After *The Great Gatsby*, our novel of manners, with a
few exceptions,[3] has tended to slickness, to recapitulating mind-
lessly certain fashionable postures about American life. Though
O'Hara has made sex a household word and consequently as
dull as dish washing and as stultifying as television, he, like such
lesser writers as Drury, Wouk, and Wallace—the names change
from year to year—is a chronicler not of real manners but of
party manners, where everyone is on his best (and worst) sociological behavior. The novel of manners has always been, with
the notable exception of Henry James, a secondary and somewhat artificial tradition in American literature, and though currently it may be dead or at least dormant, the American novel
itself is apparently thriving. Unable to believe in the surface

2 There are almost as many types of novels as there are novels themselves, and consequently when a critic breaks categories down into subtler
and more restrictive components, he is only abetting the confusion. Each
great novel creates its own category.

3 *Mrs. Bridge* (1959) by Evan S. Connell is probably the best of our
recent novels of manners, though it is, at the same time, a kind of prose
poem, treating the inner landscape as well as the outer one. Told in a
succession of poignant anecdotes, Connell's first novel is diminished to
some extent by the mediocrity of its subject, Mrs. Bridge herself. In creating Mrs. Bridge, Connell has transformed a stereotype into a real woman,
but he has been unable to make her empty life profound enough to reach
the spiritual desolation we share in common with her.

(the *Life* magazine reality) of our world, the best of the post-Second-World-War novelists have taken as their terrain the landscape of the psyche—that lonely and terrifying sanctuary where the possibilities of heroism and love and nobility comfort our fantasies.

Generalizations are approximate truths, poetic lies, but as the world is imperfect, sometimes it is necessary to lie a little to get at the truth. The contemporary American novel, one concedes, has certain blood ties with the romance. Its concerns tend to be cosmic rather than societal, its view of the world hallucinatory rather than objective, its moral alternatives metaphysical rather than practical. As in the romance, the "underside of consciousness" becomes topside, assumes the prerogatives of consciousness. Novels as remarkably different in texture and tone as Bellow's *Henderson the Rain King*, Hawkes's *Second Skin*,[4] and Burrough's *Naked Lunch* share in common a dreamlike world. Yet with the exception of some recent apocalyptic comic novels, whose characters are intentionally cartooned, the contemporary novel tends to be concerned, as the romance is only abstractly, with man (lower case m), with the extremes of human behavior. The world of the novel may be the off-center world of nightmare, but the characters who populate it—the heroes in particular—tend to be men of passion and consciousness, realistic figures, larger and more intensely real than life. In fact two of the most memorable characters in all fiction are from contemporary American novels: Bellow's Henderson and less known, the title character of Wallant's *The Pawnbroker*, Sol Nazerman.

4 Each of John Hawkes's impressively dislocated novels has a different nominal locale, yet they all seem to take place in the same timeless decayed and decaying no-land. Hawkes's surreal world is deliberately out of focus, blurred over by a fog of ugly images which we experience vaguely and unpleasantly, like, as his admirers assert, an actual nightmare. Hawkes is something of a naturalist in reverse; where the naturalist gives us the detailed surface of everyday squalid existence, Hawkes gives us with his own psychoanalytic verisimilitude the blurred surface of the workaday evil dream. His work is prescriptively contemporary, related on the one hand to the nightmare world of Flannery O'Connor and on the other to the antinovels of Sarraute and Robbe-Grillet; for all the brilliances of Hawkes's style, the novels seem so many eccentric exercises—an extraordinary game superbly played, but a game nevertheless.

The religious or cosmological preoccupation of the contemporary American novel is in part the result of the practical failure of various social utopian ideals of the twenties and thirties. The proletarian social novel of the thirties (democracy's answer to the class-conscious English novel of manners), powered by the immediacy of its concerns and the naïveté of its ideas, achieved in the works of Steinbeck, Dos Passos, and Farrell a passionate and humane journalism. However, social and political reforms, the New Deal, the existential implications of Auschwitz, Russian totalitarianism, the Un-American Activities Committee, the nuclear arms race, the Cold War, and a new critical sophistication have all collaborated to make such premature classics as *The Grapes of Wrath, USA,* and *Studs Lonigan* seem merely documents of another age. Is it possible that the Dos Passos of *Midcentury* (1961) hates FDR and the New Deal because they have deprived him of a subject, because they have nullified the protest of his earlier work? Whereas the proletarian novel of the thirties, for the most part informed by a vigorous social conscience, conceded the larger seriousness of art for the immediate seriousness of a dramatized editorial, the novel of the fifties at its best goes beneath the particular social evil to the fact of evil itself and dramatizes the extent and implications of personal culpability in a self-destroying civilization. Social wrongs are still at issue in such recent novels as *Invisible Man, All the King's Men, Catch 22, The Victim, The Prospect before Us,* and *Wise Blood,* but the question of repairing these wrongs seems nightmarishly beside the point. The rent in our lives persists unhealed by legislation.

If we have on the one hand a novel of nightmares, we have on the other—sometimes the same hand—a highly developed awareness of form, a generally impressive technical sophistication. Many a minor novelist today is a more skilled practitioner of the craft (and art) of fiction—which is not to say that he is necessarily writing better novels—than some of the major writers of the twenties and thirties. The expense, however, of an overly refined craft is that it is always in danger of becoming an end—a dead end—in itself. Sophistication polarized by narcissism can be a specious blessing. It has spawned a school of elegant fiction, quasi-decadent, quasi-innocent, which knows often more than it should but very little really worth knowing. We are, in our arts as in our sports as in our popular heroes, a country of prodigies, in which youth is often its own undenied and undeniable recommendation. So much of the mythos of American life is predicated on this apotheosis of youthful energy and its corollary that there is nothing further to learn after the first premature blush of knowledge. If energy is all, the distinction between adolescence and maturity is essentially one of vitality and depletion, life and death. A peculiar American phenomenon is that a large number of our writers seem to have been born fully grown, fully equipped, in a sense perfectly formed midgets who are replicas of great novelists in every sense but stature. Though we have lost our innocence, we have not wholly lost its illusion. We can admire the precocity of our prodigies for a time, until we discover that they are not really little boys any more but aged child impersonators (is not the ageless Peter Pan, with his cant of never growing up, really a child impersonator?), and we go on to our next child wonder, hoping that this one actually never shall grow up.

Truman Capote has been the most talented and enduring of our writers of precocious sensibility. He is a master stylist and craftsman; he writes the prose sentence at least as well as any of his contemporaries. His first and best novel, *Other Voices, Other Rooms* (1948), published at twenty-three, is a brilliant and original work. Yet when one looks behind the flashing soft-colored lights of the prose, what is the novel really about? Its ageless child-hero's loss of innocence? The boy's search for a father? His initiation into homosexuality? The narrative deals with these concerns, and to that extent they are what the novel is about. But Capote's magical stagelike world, in which Joel performs his nightmarish rite of passage, is not to be believed. It is the stuff that literary children's dreams are made of. Despite its waxwork of horrors—the paralyzed father, the girl whose throat has been cut, the lovesick dwarf, the female men, and the masculine women—there is no evil in Capote's bittersweet paradise; there is wickedness, or rather naughtiness, but that is another matter—or no matter at all. Can a novel be about anything when there is nothing real at stake? Joel doesn't fall; he is prefallen. In accepting Cousin Randolph as his father-

mother-lover, he is merely fulfilling the predefined pattern of
his fantasies. By the same token, the corrupt Randolph is also
innocent, as are all the perversities of Capote's inverted Eden.
Decadence is innocence. All is innocence. No one in the novel
is held responsible for his acts, and by and large each act is as
good, indifferent, and inevitable as another. The problem is
not that Capote's world is immoral but that among innocents
morality is beside the point. Without morality, however, the
rest, the titillating horrors of sensibility, are beside the point.

If tremulous sensibility leaves out too much, so in its own
way does the bemusement of coldly rational intelligence.
Though literacy and intelligence are distinguishing strengths of
the contemporary novel, academic detachment has also had its
disabling effects. No one contests any longer that the novel has
(despite its protean varieties) a form, or pretends that style is a
veil of gentility between the real thing and the overdelicate
reader. However, if *real* life is not the final stuff of the novel, it
is at least the first stuff. Whereas the primitive naturalists, of
whom James Jones seems to be the last bison, found and lost
life in the details of its surface, the academic novelist at his
worst is not concerned with real life but with real and unreal
ideas, with the moral of the tale and not the tale itself. He
writes literature as if it were something only technically—com-
promisingly—connected with life. He can dispense with the raw
materials of life because he has learned that they do not have
intrinsic significance. But no matter how hard he blows, he
finds it impossible to animate inorganic matter. The novel as
a form deals with human experience or with nothing at all—the
latter often dignified by scholars with the title of "allegory."
Without flesh and blood human beings in a novel, its symbolic
meanings are so many window decorations in a vacant store.

Though hardly an allegorist, Mary McCarthy is one example
of what I mean by the academic novelist. An abrasive critical intelligence and a formidably incisive prose writer, Miss
McCarthy has not written a first-rate novel. Mainly she has not
because she is unable (or unwilling) to create characters capable
of defying their maker. They are not quite like some of Robert
Penn Warren's, embodied abstractions; but for all their simula-
tion of a kind of life, they are not quite human beings either;

they are artifacts of real people. Miss McCarthy holds them up to the fluoroscope of her critical intelligence and finds them sterile and absurd, mean and pretentious, deceitful and corrupt, and worse. How comic and unpleasant we all are! And the secret is, she knew it all the time. She has schemed her characters as moral deformities in the first place. The best of her novels, *The Groves of Academe*, treats with nice comic distance the machinations of an academic failure who makes himself seem a victim of persecution in order to retain his small position in a college that seems as hypocritical, mediocre and unpleasant as the man himself. Written with a cold Augustan eye, a scrupulous aversion for mortal weakness, *Groves of Academe* is a vicious and amusing satire, unbloodied by any real traces of human behavior. For all the wit and intelligence that informs her fictional world, it is, devoid of compassion, an unlovely wasteland. And what comfort to feel superior to her people! What small, hateful comfort! It is not so much a vision of the world that Miss McCarthy gives us but an attitude, a series of rigidly preconceived attitudes, which denies her characters the limited freedom of self-motion, and in the process the possibility of discovery which is the miracle of the novel's art.

We are notoriously a culture of first (and second) book novelists who are unable to survive the chronology of growing up without the death of energy. Success, like failure, like the loss of youth, takes its toll. The expense of spirit is incalculable. It is hard to survive without recognition and so hard—so impossibly hard in its different way—to survive in this country with it. The price of success for the best of our writers is the recognition of a special and unredeemable failure. The career of Norman Mailer, though mostly exceptional, is a case in point. His first novel, *The Naked and the Dead* (1948), was overpraised for reasons having little to do with its achievement into an extraordinary popular and literary success. At twenty-five, Mailer had written, he was told, that mythic slouching beast of our popular criticism, the great American novel. Influenced by Dos Passos and Hemingway, *The Naked and the Dead* is an ambitious, panoramic, powerfully rendered realistic novel which only occasionally transcends the meaning of particular experiences—the charged raw materials of the war itself. What the novel does brilliantly is evoke the experience of war: the heat, the wet, the odors, the fear, the stupidity, the waste, the degradation, the unmitigating and unredemptive nightmare of the battlefield. As is often the case with antiwar novels, however, the impulse of *The Naked and the Dead*—its secret fascination with the violence of war—subverts the liberal high-mindedness of its intention. In the chaotic universe of war, the power drive of Mailer's villains, Croft and Cummings, seems a more positive virtue than the uncommitment of Red, the humility of Goldstein, the innocent liberalism of Hearn, or the weakness of the others, the naked and the dead.

If Mailer avoids the trap of self-imitation in his later two novels, he avoids it at the exorbitant risk of testing, with the odds contrived against him, the durability of his talent. Both *Barbary Shore* (1951) and *Deer Park* (1955) are adventurous failures, quixotic attempts at redefining the possibilities of the task. While *The Naked and the Dead* is not nearly as good as its reputation, *Barbary Shore* and *Deer Park* are not nearly as bad as theirs. Much of *Deer Park*, in fact, is Mailer at his best. Marion Faye's dope dream, the shrill Hollywood parties, the love-making of Elena and Eitel are as charged with the energy of insight as almost anything in contemporary fiction; yet other parts of the novel, especially Sergius's hallucinatory dialogue with God at the end, are incomparably, embarrassingly indulgent. It is Mailer's peculiar exhibitionistic gift to be from one moment to the next either better or worse than anyone. As with *The Naked and the Dead* and *Barbary Shore*, the point of view of *Deer Park* is not so much ambivalent as vaguely defined. What is being satirized in the novel? What is Mailer affirming? Does it matter? *Deer Park* is a curious failure; it is an alternately impressive and atrocious serious novel.

In recent years Mailer seems to have emerged as a more significant essayist than novelist—along with Baldwin, the most apocalyptic of our literate journalists. It is ironic that Mailer wrote the essays ostensibly to keep himself in the public eye while he was working on an ambitious ten-volume novel, "the longest ball ever to go up into the accelerated hurricane air of our American letters." Instead of the ten-volume marvel, we have a new one-volume novel from Mailer, serialized in *Es-*

quire, which is, if such a distinction is still possible, Mailer's most embarrassing performance to date. Yet one still believes in him. For all his posing and chest-thumping, his success-mongering and clownish self-parody, he is an authentic talent, capable at his best (as in the story "The Man Who Studied Yoga") of touching the very deepest nerves of contemporary experience. Mailer remains now, as after the publication of his first novel, a potential major novelist who has not yet written a major novel.

2

Novels are, by reason of their length and less rigorously defined requirements, more difficult to write about than poems, and, though the surface is often easier to penetrate, more difficult to read well. As Percy Lubbock has pointed out in *The Craft of Fiction*, one cannot, as with a poem, command the entire experience of a novel at once; it is too long, too diverse, too complex—in effect, because our reading of it is necessarily broken into several sittings, too fragmentary. If it is impractical to explicate a novel line-by-line, it does not necessarily follow that the critic of fiction should avoid textual analysis altogether. What does follow is that he must apply it discreetly to illuminate the most complex and crucial scenes. Novels, like poems, are made of words, and to deny the importance of language to the final achievement of a novel (as have some of Dreiser's defenders) is to under-value the weapons of prose. As technique can work discovery, prose is capable of its own illuminations. A good paragraph in a novel of Lawrence or Faulkner is likely to reveal more of the unknown world than the collected works of any number of pedestrian minor writers.

Like form and matter, style and mind are not dichotomous and consequently are only arbitrarily separable. For this reason the artificial flowers of Dreiser's prose (as opposed to the real weeds) are representative as much of a failure of intelligence as of a bad ear for language. Though the clumsily written *Sister Carrie*, for example, is because of its ambitions a more significant novel than a bonbon like *Breakfast at Tiffany's*, which sentence-by-sentence is better written, it is a less-than-great novel. It is less than great because the language is inadequate—soft-centered, banal, on the dull edge of imprecision—incapable of transmuting profound experience. Obviously, fine writing is no substitute for seriousness of purpose, but neither is drudging solemnity. As Lionel Trilling has observed, "The great novelists have usually written very good prose, and what comes through even a bad translation is exactly the power of mind that made the well-hung sentence of the original text." Style is more than just fancy dress. It is the ideal accommodation of language to the evocation of experience. Too often showy writing, which illuminates merely itself, passes for good writing; too often bad writing, which is by turns clubfooted and pretentious, is credited with being honest and profound, as if inexactness were a revelation of the ineffable.

It would be idle to say that there is only one right way of criticizing a novel, which is not to say that there are no wrong ways. On the contrary, there seem to be too many wrong ways, too many approaches which are sterile, irrelevant, self-insistent. The worst of them arrogate to their investigation the importance of that which is being investigated, as if works of literature were created only to make literary criticism, or literary-cultural history, possible. There are certain inherent presumptions in approaching literature in terms of preconceived ideology. The most notable is the tendentious expediency to manipulate the concerns of a particular novel to satisfy the terms of a general unifying construction. As R. P. Blackmur warns in "A Critic's Job of Work":

> The worse evil of fanatic falsification—of arrogant irrationality and barbarism in all its forms—arises when a body of criticism is governed by an idée fixe, a really exaggerated heresy, when a notion of genuine but small scope is taken literally to be of universal application.

The *idée fixe* becomes a kind of Procrustes' bed, deforming works of literature to make them fit the critic's predefined scheme for them—an obscene act of collaboration. Abstract critical constructions—easier perhaps to abhor than to avoid

—choke off the possibilities of discovery; they are feasible only as a suggestive device, as a starting point of explication, a way to get into a novel and not out of it.

Similarly, a novel should not be discussed, as it generally is in academic journals, solely in terms of its ideation, as if ideas were all it were about. An analysis of the meanings that inform the experience of a novel is not an invalid concern, but it is not the whole concern; nor is it, I suspect, even the primary one. Arid novels are often misrepresented and dignified by critical ingenuities, by explication-in-a-vacuum, which assumes (though actual evaluation is usually avoided) that the quality of a work's abstractable ideas is indicative of its importance. There is, of course, a relationship between the quality of ideas that inform a novel and its final achievement as literature, but it is a subtler and more tenuous connection than the ideational critics allow. The only meanings in a novel that count are those that come out of the rendered experience. Therefore, to talk about a novel with any sense of completeness, the critic must come to terms somehow with the texture and import of its experience. I am aware that this can lead to the worst kind of murky private criticism, while there is less danger with pure explication in which ideas can be abstracted from a novel—at least intentional ideas—with reasonable accuracy. Yet if a novel does not generate an experience, it has no ideas, at least none worth talking about. If criticism is to transcend mediocrity, it must, like art, risk being bad in order to be good.

Generally, critical books dealing with a group of novelists tend to treat individual works cursorily in order to be able within a limited space to evaluate the over-all achievement of each writer concerned. Given the scope of its purpose, this method has genuine practical advantages. But if one is concerned primarily with literature and not literary history or literary biography, the method has certain esthetic liabilities. It requires us to forego the insides of novels for their outsides. There is a direct correspondence: the more inclusive the general coverage, the less intensive the analysis of particular novels. The converse is also true. In the first extreme, one

often cannot see a particular novel for the literary woods; in
the second, one sees, perhaps, only individual novels. It is idle
to say that one method is better than the other; they each
serve different purposes. It is my contention, however, that if
a novel is worth analyzing, it is worth analyzing intensively. As
a case in point, Dorothy Van Ghent's *The English Novel,
Form and Function*, which treats individual novels in depth,
is a more insightful, if less generally informative, work than
Walter Allen's more or less inclusive critical history, *The
English Novel*. Ultimately, Mrs. Van Ghent's book, because
it tells us more about particular English novels, tells us more
about the English novel.

Rather than investigate in brief, then, the major work of
nearly all of the serious or quasi-serious post-Second-World-
War American novelists, I have limited myself to a close
analysis of nine novels. My choice of writers has been governed
largely by two concerns: to treat the most significant of the
serious novels and to represent the range and quality of seriousness of the fiction of the period. I have conspicuously omitted
discussions of the work of certain currently fashionable reputa-
tions for which I plead (arrogantly) the limitations of taste.
For reasons of focus, I have avoided treating writers who have
written creditable novels in the past eighteen years but whose
main body of work was written before 1945. Though I am
more concerned with novels than novelists, I have omitted
discussions, with two exceptions which I think explain themselves, of individually interesting works by novelists who have
produced little else, or little else of value. My justification for
this rather arbitrary circumscription is that we have in this
Peter Pan culture a superabundance of promising first novels
and that, to some extent, I am also concerned with the
achievement and potential achievement of the novelist.

I have chosen to concentrate my discussion on Robert Penn
Warren's *All the King's Men* (1946), Saul Bellow's *The Victim* (1947), J. D. Salinger's *The Catcher in the Rye* (1951),
Ralph Ellison's *Invisible Man* (1953), Flannery O'Connor's
Wise Blood (1952), Bernard Malamud's *The Assistant*
(1957), William Styron's *Lie Down in Darkness* (1951), Edward Lewis Wallant's *The Pawnbroker* (1961), and Wright

Morris' *Ceremony in Lone Tree* (1960).[5] If one had to abstract from these novels a unifying concern, a characteristic serious-ness, it would be Dostoevskian, the confrontation of man with the objectification of his primordial self and his exemplary spiritual passage from innocence to guilt to redemption. This theme of guilt and redemption, because of its centrality and resonance, seems to me a useful critical focus with which to approach what I believe to be the most significant of the post-Second-World-War American novels.

[5] I have no doubt that I have omitted writers who might have been selected over several on this list (James Baldwin, Norman Mailer, James Purdy, John Hawkes, William Burroughs, and so on) and that, with the added perspective of say ten years, my choice of novels may seem perverse if not arbitrary. Yet if the nine works I have selected are not the best of the post-Second-World-War novels, they are at least illustra-tive of the kind and quality of seriousness of the fiction of the period.

2 · The Metaphysics of Demagoguery:
All the King's Men by Robert Penn Warren

ALTHOUGH Robert Penn Warren is a generation or so older than, with one exception, any of the writers treated in this study, he is technically a post-Second-World-War novelist. That is, the larger body of his fiction, including his major novel *All the King's Men*, has been published since 1945. Though a valuable novelist, Warren is also notably a playwright, poet, teacher, scholar, and critic—a man of letters in the best sense. The problem is, how does a man write a novel unself-consciously, when he is aware just how the critic, created perhaps in his own image, is likely to read it? The answer is, he doesn't. At least Warren doesn't.

Almost all of Warren's fiction suffers somewhat from the determined this-marriage-can-be-saved compatibility between Warren the novelist and Warren the explicator. The harder he tries to fuse the two selves, the farther apart they spring, as if resistant to the meddling of an outsider. As Eric Bentley has actually observed, "The problem lies precisely in his [Warren's] being so two-sidedly gifted; he evidently finds it endlessly difficult to combine his two sorts of awareness." Warren's novels are informed by a fairly complex set of intellectual alternatives, while at the same time they rely for their movement on frenetically charged melodramatic action, often for its own sake, for the sake merely of narrative excitement. Though Warren is a serious novelist, and at his best a brilliant prose writer, there is a curious separation in his novels between the events of the narrative and the meaning Warren insists they accommodate.

Of Warren's eight novels to date, *All the King's Men* (1946) seems to me the most achieved, the most serious and the most enduring—for all its flaws, one of our near-great novels. For some time *All the King's Men* was misread as a disturbingly sympathetic fictionalized account of the demagogic career of Huey Long. Approached as an historical document, the book was condemned by politically liberal critics as a florid, rhetorical justification for a Napoleonic brand of American neo-fascism. There is no need any longer to point out the irrelevancy of this attack, to explain that Jack Burden is the center of the novel and that Willie Stark, "the man of fact," is not *actually* Huey Long, but a kind of "Mistah Kurtz." In fact, in recent years a critical orthodoxy has clustered about Warren's novels, which is not unlike those contemporary angels headed by C. S. Lewis and Douglas Bush who guard the gates around Milton's *Paradise Lost*, protecting it from profanation by the infernal satanists. In both cases the defense is warranted; there is a real enemy. But in both cases the enemy is already within the gates. Though Warren intends Jack Burden to be the center of the novel, Willie Stark is by virtue of his energy the more realized and interesting character. Burden, as thinly disguised authorial spokesman, is a literary conception, created from other fiction rather than from life, a combination, if you can imagine it, of Nick Carraway and Sam Spade. Whatever Warren's intention, the character of Willie Stark, a colossus of human and inhuman possibilities, inadvertently dominates the novel. Inevitably, a distortion results, the kind of distortion which would permit *All the King's Men* to be read as the story of Willie Stark's rise and fall (a tragedy of over-reaching pride brought low by retributive justice).

For all that, Jack Burden, acquiescent narrator, at once vicarious Willie and vicarious Adam, is the novel's center, the ultimate synthesizer of its polarities. While Willie and Adam die unfulfilled, Jack completes the spiritual voyage; he moves, an exemplary sleepwalker, from sin to recognition and guilt to redemption and rebirth. Jack's ritual search for a true father, or at least a true absolute, leads him into Willie's employ (on the coat-tails of his political ascension). Ironically, there is a certain amount of narcissism in Jack's discipleship because he has, in part, created Willie the "Boss," catalyzed him from the raw materials of "Cousin Willie from the country." At the outset, Willie is an innocent, a do-gooder whose campaign speeches are scrupulously honest and drearily dull. Jack gives him his first taste of the apple:

"Hell, make 'em cry, make 'em laugh, make 'em think you're God-Almighty. Or make 'em mad. Even mad at you. Just stir 'em up, it doesn't matter how or why, and they'll love you and come back for more. Pinch them in the soft place. They aren't alive, most of 'em haven't been alive in twenty years. Hell, their wives have lost their teeth and their shape, and likker won't set on their stomachs, and they don't believe in God, so it's up to you to give 'em something to stir 'em up and make 'em feel again. . . . But for Sweet Jesus' sake don't try to improve their minds." [1]

This is the first and last time that Jack gives Willie a short course in cynical wisdom.[2] Once having learned the lesson, Willie becomes the teacher, the authority on man's fallen nature. As Willie tells Jack later on in his (and Warren's) characteristic evangelical rhetoric: " 'Man is conceived in sin and born in corruption and passeth from the stink of the didie to the stench of the shroud. There is always something' " (p. 157).

It is Jack, however, who has initiated Willie's conversion from the man of idea to the man of fact, from romanticism to pragmatism. By demonstrating to him that his start in politics was made possible by political corruption, Jack destroys Willie's sense of innocence, decreates him into manhood. While Jack, who suffers chronically from paralysis of the will, converts Willie through abstract example, Willie converts the uncommitted Jack through practical demonstration. The "Boss" Willie is Jack as he would like to be, but only if he could watch himself being it. For all his admiration of action, Jack is essentially a spectator, an historian waiting for history to happen. Willie performs history for him, tests the efficacy of Jack's theories, while Jack with clinical dispassion sits on the sidelines taking

1 Robert Penn Warren, *All the King's Men* (New York: Harcourt, Brace & World, Inc., 1946), p. 72. All quotations are from this edition.
2 Taken out of context, this passage could conceivably pass for one of Willie's own speeches.

notes. (Jack's role as spectator is defined symbolically in the scene in which he sits in the hospital amphitheatre watching Adam Stanton perform a lobotomy.) As a dutiful son, Jack Burden participates in and even admires his father's ruthless pragmatism without sensing his own culpability. What you refuse to know can't hurt you, but, as Jack discovers, for only so long as you can remain blind. The longer you avoid self-knowledge, however, the more vulnerable you are to its intrusion.

Aside from Willie, Jack has two other fathers: a nominal one who he thinks is real and whom he has rejected (Ellis Burden) and a real one whom he admires and inadvertently kills (Judge Irwin). When Willie assigns him to get "something on" Judge Irwin, who has been outspoken in his criticism of Stark's administration, Jack is forced for the first time to choose between the prerogatives of opposing fathers. (Though he doesn't know that Irwin is his natural father, he respects, resents, and feels obligated to Irwin as a son to a father because of Irwin's decency and friendship over the years.) Looking for a way out of his predicament, Jack tells Willie that Irwin is "washed in the blood" and that an investigation of Irwin's past will be a waste of time. Willie knows, however, that man is fallen, that "there is always something." In investigating the facts of Irwin's life, Jack puts to the test the last illusion he has permitted himself to retain, that despite the rank and malodorous corruption which underlies so much of contemporary life, a truly good man like Irwin remains incorruptible. Jack has another naïve notion which justifies the political dirt-digging he does so that Willie can blackmail his opponents: that the truth, regardless of its immediate effects, is always salutary and that unadulterated fact constitutes truth.

In search of the hidden facts of his real father's past, Jack visits Ellis Burden, the Scholarly Attorney turned Religious fanatic, his nominal father. It is here that the divergent influences of his trinity of fathers come into focus and are symbolically defined. Once again, Jack rejects the Scholarly Attorney, the weak saint, whose life of squalor, piety, and undiscriminating compassion seems purposeless to him when contrasted with Willie Stark's vigorous usefulness. This dispossessed nominal father has adopted a substitute son, George, a former circus aerialist who has reverted to childhood. George, redeemed through trauma into helpless innocence, spends his time making angels from masticated bread crusts. He is, in an ironic sence, Jack's brother. George's idiot purity embarrasses Jack and he rejects the image of his opposite (his innocent brother) along with his Scholarly Attorney father, along with the past. But, at the same time, he is again rejected by his father, who refuses to answer his questions about Irwin—who is unable to hear him when Jack calls him "Father." The visit is a failure; Jack learns nothing about Irwin, and he experiences the loss of his father all over again.

The uncovering of Irwin's one dishonorable act has massive, unaccountable ramifications. In consequence of Jack's discovery, Judge Irwin commits suicide, Anne Stanton has a self-destructive affair with Willie Stark, Adam Stanton kills Willie Stark, and Willie Stark's bodyguard kills Adam Stanton. For all his disinterested intentions, Jack must bear the burden of responsibility for this proliferation of tragedy. He has set it in motion as surely and perfectly as if he had consciously planned it. The "facts" that incriminate the Judge also indicate the complicity of Governor Stanton, who deliberately covered up for his friend. This further discovery destroys for both Anne and Adam Stanton the idealized notion of their father that has sustained them in their myth of purity as children of innocence—descendants of innocence. When Anne discovers that the purity of the old governor is tainted, she is able to shed her restrictive moral restraints as a snake sheds its skin. If there is no pure God, a pure Satan is the next best thing—he is at least whole. With the loss of her good father, Anne commits a sort of symbolic incest with the bad father—the new governor—searching for an absolute to replace the one she had lost. The loss of innocence in the novel for Jack, Willie, Anne, and Adam is concomitant with the loss of the good father.

It is Adam, Jack's innocent self, the least convincing of all Warren's characters, who guilelessly gives Jack his first lead in uncovering Irwin's blemished past. Adam answers Jack's cunning, direct question, "Was Judge Irwin ever broke?" because he is too ingenuous not to. However, Adam's innocent volunteering of harmless information about Judge Irwin is, in its effects, irresponsible as only innocence can be. It gives Jack the necessary clue to unearth Irwin's guilty secret, which, in ramification, destroys each of the participants in the central action of the novel. Adam's ingenuousness here anticipates his later, more destructive, act of innocence—his self-righteous assassination of Willie Stark. To say any more about Adam is beside the point. Whereas some of Warren's characters are half-human, half-idea, Adam is pure idea; he is an allegorical personification of *Innocence*. But without life, he is finally nothing, a figment of the author's imagination.

All of Warren's main characters experience at one time or another the loss of innocence and are characterized in terms of their accommodation to their Fall. Judge Irwin, sustained like Adam by the myth of self-purity, has attempted to evade the implications of his one intentionally corrupt act (his Fall) by shutting it out of his memory. Some thirty years later, Jack, the unacknowledged child of his loins, confronts him with the forgotten past. Jack's confrontation has a twofold significance; Jack is the manifestation of Irwin's other sin, his adulterous affair with Jack's mother, so that he becomes for Irwin the symbol of his fallen past, the tale-bearer of one crime and the embodiment of the other. Warren images Jack's information as a barb finding meat, suggesting its lethal nature. The Judge, illuminated by self-knowledge at once destructive and redemptive, bears his pain stoically. For a moment Irwin is tempted to reveal to his son the nature of their relationship in order that Jack withhold his information, but he doesn't—because it is beside the point.

"I wouldn't hurt you," he said. Then, reflectively, added, "But I could stop you."
"By stopping MacMurfee," I said.
"A lot easier than that."
"How?"
"A lot easier than that," he repeated.
"How?"
"I could just . . ." he began, "I could just say to you—I could just tell you something. . . ." He stopped then suddenly rose to his feet, spilling the papers off his knees. "But I won't," he said cheerfully and smiled directly at me. [p. 347]

The moment of recognition is averted. By not telling Jack—an act of moral restraint—Irwin accepts full responsibility for his sin. Irwin's withholding of his "truth" is, given the occasion, more honorable than Jack's revelation of his. The next morning Jack is awakened by his mother's "bright, beautiful silvery soprano screams." In her hysteria, she continues to shriek at Jack, "You killed him. You killed him," without identifying the "him": "'Killed who?' I demanded, shaking her. 'Your father,' she said, 'your father and oh! you killed him'" (p. 350).

Without further clarification, Jack realizes what has happened, as if he had known all the time, in the secret wisdom of instinct, that Irwin was his father. That the Judge shoots himself through the heart indicates symbolically the implication of Jack's betrayal. Despite the terrible consequences of his act, Jack reflects on his responsibility for Irwin's suicide, as if it were an intellectual abstraction which does not touch him personally. At first he considers his father's death as the just retribution of Mortimer Littlepaugh, the man whom Irwin's own corrupt act drove to suicide. Then:

Or had it been Mortimer? Perhaps I had done it. That was one way of looking at it. I turned that over and speculated upon my responsibility. It would be quite possible to say that I had none, no more than Mortimer had. Mortimer had killed Judge Irwin because Judge Irwin had killed him and I killed Judge Irwin because Judge Irwin had created me, and looking at matters in that light one could say that Mortimer and I were only the twin instruments of Irwin's protracted and ineluctable self-destruction. For either killing or creating may be a crime punishable by death, and the death always comes by the criminal's own hand and every man is a suicide. If a man knew how to live he would never die. [p. 353]

It is a characteristically easy rationalization for Jack, one which enables him to avoid for a time the implications of his behavior. Like every man, he too is a suicide (though a moral rather than a physical one) and, ultimately, ineluctably, his sins revisit him like retributive ghosts. As a result of Irwin's death, Jack loses two fathers, the weak but saintly Scholarly Attorney and the strong but tainted judge. Willie Stark, the evil father, the father who has cuckolded him, is all that is left for Jack in a world of decimated fathers, and finally Jack kills him too. As Jack tells us, "'I had dug up the truth and the truth always

kills the father.' " In a symbolic sense, only after Jack destroys
his fathers can he become a man himself. As part of his quest
for knowledge (manhood), Jack kills the fathers of his world
only to resurrect them finally in himself.

Jack's articulated intellection dissipates the effect of this
scene as it does much of the richly rendered experience of the
novel. Granted his cleverness, Jack is verbally aware of too
much, and also too little; Warren is forever peeking over his
shoulder, but withholding from his narrator the whole picture.
That Jack as narrator is almost always the deception of an insight ahead of the reader is one of the recurring distractions of
the novel. With rare exception, the reader is not permitted to
discover meanings; they are discovered for him.

When Willie loses his innocence, he is transformed almost
overnight from the son of his world to its father. Willie's
spiritual metamorphosis (which resembles Kurtz's in *Heart of
Darkness*), though thematically subordinate to Jack's guilt-and-
redemption passage, dominates the action of the novel. Willie's
career anticipates and parallels Jack's, as a father's anticipates a
son's, though it is enlarged where Jack's is diminished, and
Willie never successfully makes the spiritual voyage back from
hell. Like Kurtz, the "Boss" has gone too far into darkness
ever to return into light.

Willie becomes governor. Ostensibly, his ends have not
changed, only his means of achieving them. Gradually, however,
the ends become inseparable from their means and Willie yields
himself to his most voracious interior devils. The thesis is
classic and bromidic: power tends to corrupt; absolute power
tends to corrupt absolutely. With a difference, however:
Warren inverts the cliché; for all his sins, "Willie is a great
man." This is the verdict of his wife Lucy, to whom he has
been unfaithful, whose son he has destroyed through vanity, and
of Jack Burden, whom he has disillusioned and nearly destroyed.
Since the redeemed Jack Burden, who has moved from blindness to whole sight represents, one must believe, the point of
view of the novel, this must stand as Warren's judgment of
Stark. The question remains: Is it a reasonable judgment borne
out by the experience of the novel? Or is it a piece of gratuitous
iconoclasm, the cliché-anti-cliché?

Warren enlists sympathy for Willie by indicating that the context in which he is forced to operate (southern politics) is unreclaimably corrupt. Whereas Tiny Duffy and Willie's opponent MacMurfee are interested in petty graft as an end, Willie's ego wants nothing less than recognition by posterity. Willie is a real devil at sup among dwarfed, flabby devils; in that he is more real and more potent than the others, he is to that extent more admirable. Once Willie has fallen, he discovers his true voice, the voice of the rabble rouser, the appeal to primordial violence:

"You asked me what my program is. Here it is, you hicks. And don't you forget it. Nail 'em up! Nail up Joe Harrison. Nail up anybody who stands in your way. Nail up MacMurfee if he don't deliver. You hand me the hammer and I'll do it with my own hand. Nail 'em up on the barn door." [p. 96]

The easier it becomes for Willie to manipulate the crowd, the less respect he has for its common fallen humanity. As he becomes more powerful, he becomes, like Kurtz and like Macbeth, more voracious, more proud, more evil. Willie's palpable moral decline is manifested for us when he covers up for an underling who has taken graft. It is not in the act of covering up but in his justification for it that Willie's inhumanity and presumption are manifested:

"My God, you talk like Byram was human! He's a thing! You don't prosecute an adding machine if a spring goes bust and makes a mistake. You fix it. Well, I fixed Byram. I fixed Byram. I fixed him so his unborn great-grandchildren will wet their pants on this anniversary and not know why. Boy, it will be the shock in the genes. Hell, Byram is just something you use, and he'll sure be useful from now on." [p. 136]

Willie's self-defining presumption is that he *knows* himself a superior being, aspiring to law, to omnipotence, to God. The machine metaphor he employs reveals his attitude not only toward Byram but toward the populace in general: people are things to be used by him, "the Boss," for *his* purposes. From Willie's "bulging-eyed" point-of-view, everything, all existence, has been set in motion to serve him.

Willie's will to power, his lust for omnipotence, is defeated by what might be called a tragic virtue. Despite Willie's professed thesis that "you have to make the good out of the bad because that's all you have to make it out of," that all men are innately corrupt, that "political graft is the grease that keeps the wheels from squeaking," he wants to build a magnificent, immaculate hospital as his gift to the state, untainted by the usual petty corruption and graft. In pursuing this ideal, Willie refuses a deal with Gummy Larson, the power behind his enemy MacMurfee, whose defection to Willie would leave the "Boss" all but unopposed. Having fallen from Paradise into Hell, Willie wishes—his one romantic illusion—to regain his lost purity, to buy back Paradise. Willie tries to explain his motives to Jack:

> "Can't you understand either? I'm building that place, the best in the country, the best in the world, and a bugger like Tiny is not going to mess with it, and I'm going to call it the Willie Stark Hospital and it will be there a long time after I'm dead and gone and you are dead and gone and all those sons-of-bitches are dead and gone and anybody, no matter he hasn't got a dime, can go there . . ."
> "And will vote for you," I said.
> "I'll be dead," he said, "and you'll be dead, and I don't care whether he votes for me or not, he can go there and . . ."
> "And bless your name," I said. [p. 233]

That Willie, so compellingly articulate on other occasions, cannot cogently rationalize his motives suggests that they are contradictory to him as well as to Jack. He wants at once to be noble and to have everyone admire his nobility—selflessness for the sake of self. Yet, and herein lies the contradiction, he also wants redemption.

As part of his obsessive desire to transcend his corruption, his dream of greatness, Willie hires Adam Stanton to run his hospital, hoping through connection, through transfusion of spirit, to inform himself with Adam's innocence. Ironically, Willie has, with almost perfect instinct, chosen his redeemer, his redeemer as executioner. Adam and Willie as ideological polarities must inevitably merge or destroy each other. Jack unites them; he is the means of their collaborative self-destruction.

Willie's brief affair with Adam's sister Anne, is another extension of his specious quest for innocence. What Willie pursues is not innocence, really, but seeming innocence—respectability. His holy search for the false grail is the tragic flaw in his otherwise perfect expediency. Willie's lost innocence resides not with Adam and Anne, but with his wife Lucy and his father; his substitution of Anne for Lucy symbolizes his degeneration, his spiritual blindness. In his obsession with purity, Willie makes an enemy of the spiteful Tiny Duffy and puts too much faith in the erratically naïve, the fallen innocent, Adam, thereby predicating his own destruction. Duffy makes an anonymous phone call to Adam, falsifying the implications of Anne's affair with Willie. The inflexibly idealistic Adam, unable to live in an imperfect world, acts as the unwitting tool of vengeful petty corruption and gratuitously murders Willie. Specious innocence and cowardly corruption conspire to destroy the "Boss" at the height of his power and at the threshold of his apparent self-reform.

Willie's deathbed scene is the most potent of the various dramatic climaxes in the novel. In it Warren brings sharply into focus the moral paradox of Willie's ethic—the tragedy of his unachieved, over-reaching ambition; it is rendered as Judge Irwin's death is not, as a profoundly affecting experience. It is the death of Jack's last symbolic father—in extension of all his fathers—leaving him, for a time, alone and uncommitted in the chaos of his ungoverned universe. I quote the scene at length because it is a resonant fusion of idea and action, a moment of illumined truth.[3]

For a minute he didn't speak but his eyes looked up at me, with the light still flickering in them. Then he spoke: "Why did he do it to me?"

"Oh, God damn it," I burst out, very loud, "I don't know."

The nurse looked warningly at me.

"I never did anything to him," he said.

"No, you never did."

He was silent again, and the flicker went down in his eyes. Then, "He was all right, the Doc."

I nodded.

3 I would like to believe that the truth of a serious work of art is a partial illumination of an ultimately incomprehensible mystery. When the truths of a novel are too conclusive, they are often not truths at all but, at best, popular accommodations.

I waited, but it began to seem that he wasn't going to say any more. His eyes were on the ceiling and I could scarcely tell that he was breathing. Finally, the eyes turned toward me again, very slowly, and I almost thought that I could hear the tiny painful creak of the balls in their sockets. But the light flickered up again. He said "It might have been all different, Jack."

I nodded again.

He roused himself more. He even seemed to be straining to lift his head from the pillow. "You got to believe that," he said hoarsely.

The nurse stepped forward and looked significantly at me.

"Yes," I said to the man on the bed.

"You got to," he said again. "You got to believe that."

"All right."

He looked at me, and for a moment it was the old strong, prob-ing, demanding glance. But when the words came this time, they were very weak. "And it might have been different yet," he whis-pered. "If it hadn't happend, it might—have been different—even yet." [p.400]

Willie's deathbed claim is an easy one to make; it is as im-possible to prove as to disprove. One is tempted to say to him, as Jake does to Brett at the end of *The Sun Also Rises*, "Isn't it pretty to think so?" though significantly Jack does not. How-ever, it is not out of motives of sentiment that Jack withholds his ironic disbelief. He is not fully convinced that Willie's self-justification is unjust. The possibility remains: "It might have been different—even yet." Willie is, after all, a paradox.

In becoming Willie's executioner, Adam, in his blind way, follows the example of Willie's career—he becomes Willie. For the "man of fact" and the "man of idea," as Jack classified them, there has been an alternation of roles. Each incomplete, seeking completeness, has chosen his polar opposite as an ex-emplary image. In building the hospital without the "grease" of political graft, Willie is operating idealistically—in Adam's image. In brutally shooting down Willie, Adam is acting as disciple of the man whose power-authority is symbolized by the meat axe. From Jack's standpoint, Willie is superior to Adam: "A man's virtue may be but the defect of his desire, as his crime may be but a function of his virtue." If a man has not faced temptation, or, as in Adam's case, has not admitted its existence, his purity is illusory and beside the point.

Willie's relationship to his son Tom is another variation on the novel's father-son conflict, and it serves as an ironic comment both on Jack's relationship to his real father and to Willie. Jack's search into Irwin's discreditable past is continually juxtaposed to scenes of Willie worshipfully watching Tom perform on the football field: " 'He's my boy—and there's not any like him—he'll be All-American. . . .' " Tom Stark is the perfect physical extension of Willie's wishful self-image; he is all man of action—with the bottle, on the gridiron, and in bed —one hundred percent performance, no waste. Burden sees his as "one hundred and eighty pounds of split-second, hair trigger, Swiss-watch beautiful mechanism." Inhuman but perfect, he is the embodiment of Willie's crass values. Willie is willing to overlook Tom's personal decay so long as he continues to function as a perfect mechanism on the football field and so sate Willie's rapacious vanity. Willie's attitude toward Tom is symbolic of his attitude toward the governmental machine—proud, permissive, and blind. Corruption is permissible because it "keeps the wheels from squeaking." His failure with Tom is symptomatic of his potential failure as governor; to satisfy his vanity Willie would have all men, even his own son, made into functioning "things." Inadvertently, Willie destroys Tom, who is, outside of personal power, the "thing" he loves most in his world. When Tom has been barred from playing football for breaking college rules (the boy manages, among his heroics, to cripple one girl in an auto crash and to impregnate another), Willie pressures the coach into reinstating him. Almost immediately after Tom comes into the game, as if in direct consequence of Willie's corrupt use of authority, his spine is snapped by a vicious tackle. As a result, the son of the man-of-action is left actionless, without the use of his arms and legs. As the emotional paralysis of Jack catalyzes, in a sense, the action of Willie, Willie's action causes the physical paralysis of Tom. The irony is evident: ultimately a machine stops, even a perfect Swiss-made mechanism breaks down if it is dropped too often. The sins of the father are visited on the son. Similarly, the "breaking" of the son anticipates the destruction of the father; it is an intimation of Willie's mortality.

Whereas in Jack's case the son kills the father, in Willie's the father kills the son. However, Tom is, through the ineluctable chain of cause and effect, also the instrument of Willie's destruction. As a consequence of Tom's impregnating the daughter of one of MacMurfee's men, Willie is forced through blackmail to compromise his principles and give the corrupt Gummy Larson the hospital-construction contract. After Tom's injury, however, the guilt-ridden Willie breaks the contract. Tiny Duffy, who has been intermediary in the deal, exacts his vengeance; he initiates Willie's murder through Adam's pride.

Before Adam shoots him down, Willie accepts Tom's paralysis as a judgment for his sins and seeks expiation through good works: "you got to start somewhere." As Irwin ultimately redeems Jack, Tom almost redeems Willie, but not quite; after his fall, Humpty-Dumpty cannot be put together again. Willie, like Tom's paralyzed body, is denied rebirth. Willie's death does, however, make possible the redemption of Tom's illegitimate son, whom Lucy decides to adopt and name, of all names, Willie Stark. Through his son's son, Willie regains his lost innocence.

With the death of Willie, the effective father, Jack has no one left to whom he can transfer his responsibility. However, before he can achieve manhood, Jack has one other father with whom he has to come to terms—Cass Mastern; the subject of his Ph.D. dissertation is Jack's historic father. The episode of Cass Mastern, a self-contained short story within the novel, is intended as a gloss (in Warren's term, "the myth") on the larger action of the main narrative. Though it illuminates certain themes in *All the King's Men* and is in itself an exceptionally resonant tale, Cass's tragedy is hardly indispensable to the novel. In any event, at the cost of temporarily stopping the action, it gives added dimension to Burden's odyssey into self-knowledge, his passage from innocence to limbo to guilt to redemption. Though Jack has pieced together all the facts of Cass Mastern's life, he is unable to complete his dissertation. The significance of Cass's story eludes him, though he is aware that it has significance. Neither Jack's early philosophic idealism ("What you don't know won't hurt you") nor his disillusioned belief in the Great Twitch (that man is an involuntary mechanism and no one is responsible for anything) is adequate to a comprehension of Cass's sainthood. Cass, though innocent and virtuous, falls into an affair with Annabelle Trice, his best friend's wife. As a consequence, three lives are destroyed. Thereafter Cass, suffused with guilt, makes his existence a continuous penance for his sin. He finally joins the southern army and gives up his life while refusing to fire a shot in his own defense. Through martydom he achieves expiation. At the end, Cass becomes a religious fanatic, and on his deathbed he sends a strange letter to his successful brother. The passage is typical of the evangelical eloquence of Warren's rhetoric:

> Remember me, but without grief. If one of us is lucky, it is I. I shall have rest and I hope in the mercy of the Everlasting and his blessed election. But you, my dear brother, are condemned to eat bread in bitterness and build on the place where the charred embers and ashes are and to make bricks without straw and to suffer in the ruin and guilt of our dear Land and in the common guilt of man. [p. 162]

Cass's martyrdom is exemplary; it is not only his own guilt for which he has suffered and died but the guilt of the land, "the common guilt of man." In the mystery of Cass's life and death resides the meaning of Jack's life, which is to say the essential meaning of all our lives. As Cass has written in his journal, and as Jack finally discovers for himself, " 'It is a human defect—to try to know oneself by the self of another. One can only know oneself in God and His great eye.' " After the recognition of his guilt, it is in God that Cass does find himself; similarly, after Jack accepts his guilt, it is in himself that he finds Cass and, ultimately, God. The recognition of guilt for Cass (and by implication for Jack) is an awesome discovery.

> It was, instead, the fact of all these things—the death of my friend, the betrayal of Phoebe, the suffering and rage and great change of the woman I had loved—all had come from my single act of sin and perfidy, as the boughs from the bole and the leaves from the bough. Or to figure the matter differently, it was as though the vibration set up in the whole fabric of the world by my act had spread infinitely and with ever increasing power and no man could know the end. I did not put it into words in such fashion, but I stood there shaken by a tempest of feeling. [p. 178]

Cass's revelation is existential; that is, since the ramifications of a particular act are for the most part unknowable and the inherent responsibility for its entire chain reaction inescapable, the burden of guilt is endless—and unbearable. So Cass, in search of redemption, tracks down the various consequences of his act of sin only to discover that there is no undoing of the harm he has already caused. What he has done is irrevocable. It is only by "living in God's eye"—a saint's life—that he can hope to achieve expiation and redemption.

Since Duncan Trice, who is considerably older than Cass, initiates him into vice, he is, in effect, the father of Cass's adultery with Annabelle. What Cass has learned from Duncan he had put into practice with Duncan's wife. Therefore, Cass's crime, Warren suggests, is implicitly incestuous, for if Duncan, the man whose death he effects, is his "substitute" father, Annabelle as his wife is a sort of symbolic mother. This is essentially what Cass understands when he proclaims himself " 'the chief of sinners and a plague spot on the body of the human world.' "

Cass's experience acts as an anticipatory parallel to Jack's own nightmare passage, though the connections are remote and abstract. When Jack discovers that Duffy "had killed Stark as surely as though his own hand had held the revolver," he feels absolved of responsibility, free at last to act, to vindicate the deaths of Willie and Adam. However, Jack's newborn sense of freedom is illusory. It is for him another evasion of responsibility, in a way the least admirable of all. Convincing himself as Willie had, and as Adam had when he squeezed the trigger, that an act is a self-willed moral entity, Jack assumes for himself the role of avenging angel; he wishes to destroy Duffy in order to justify himself. However, after Jack chastises Duffy, " 'You are the stinkingest louse God ever let live!' " and threatens him with exposure, he realizes that " 'I had tried to make Duffy into a scapegoat for me and to set myself off from Duffy,' " that Duffy is his alter ego, his corrupt brother, and that whatever he had said about Duffy was also true of himself. In the power of Warren's prose, we get the visceral horror of Jack's self-revulsion:

> It was as though in the midst of the scene Tiny Duffy had slowly and like a brother winked at me with his oyster eye and I had known he knew some nightmare truth, which was that we were twins bound together more intimately and disastrously than the

poor freaks of the midway who are bound by the common stitch of flesh and gristle and the seepage of blood. We are bound together forever and I could never hate him without hating myself or love myself without loving him.

And I heaved and writhed like the ox or the cat, and the acid burned my gullet and that's all there was to it and I hated everybody and myself and Tiny Duffy and Willie Stark and Adam Stanton. [p. 417]

Jack, by evading the responsibility for his own sins, had, amid the corruption about him, retained the illusion of innocence. Since he had not acted out of conscious choice, but had merely yielded to the demands of the "Boss," he had been able to slough off the burden of guilt. Once he discovers himself free to act, he becomes aware that the possibility of all acts, the whole spectrum of good and evil, are in him; that he is, as human being, Oedipus and Duffy and Willie and everyone else. Having discovered the magnitude of his guilt—that he is responsible not only for his own sins but for all sins—Jack begins his return from the interior hell in which he has languished so long. He cannot leave hell, of course, until he has discovered its boundaries.

When Jack runs into "Sugar Boy," Willie's driver and bodyguard (*the* man of action), he is presented with the opportunity of destroying Duffy with no risk to himself. He restrains himself not out of the paralysis ("the defect of desire") which prevented him many years before from making love to Anne when she offered herself to him but because Duffy is his "twin," and if he can sanction Duffy's murder he must sanction his own. (Cass refused to kill in the Civil War because: " 'How can I, who have taken the life of my friend, take the life of an enemy, for I have used up my right to blood?' ") Jack's refusal to take easy vengeance on Duffy is not inaction but a decisive moral act.

For a time, as a projection of his self-hate, Jack has a baleful view of all humanity. When he comes to love his mother, whom he has rejected long ago, he is able as a consequence to stop hating himself, which also means no longer hating the rest of the world. The redemption of his mother through the recognition of her love for Irwin (his real father) is Jack's salvation; it re-establishes for him the existential possibility of love. However, as Jack discovers, the process has been circular, for " 'by killing my father I have saved my mother's soul.' " This discovery leads Jack into a further revelation (which is Warren's thesis) that " 'all knowledge that is worth anything is maybe paid for by blood.' "

For all his belief in the purgative powers of knowledge, Jack lies to his mother when she asks about the motive for Irwin's suicide, telling her that his father killed himself because of failing health. It is, however, a salutary lie, the least he can do for his mother. As his mother's rebirth has resurrected him, Jack's lie resurrects the image of his father for his mother. (Jack's withholding of the truth from his mother closely parallels Marlowe's lie to Kurtz's intended at the end of *Heart of Darkness*. In both cases the lie is noble, and, in a sense, the truth.) His reconciliation with his mother begins his reconciliation with the past. For without the past Jack cannot really participate in the world of the present. By rediscovering the past he is able to re-create the present, to be spiritually reborn into a world in which before his destructive self-awareness he had only acquiescently participated. He moves into his father's house, affirming his linear heritage, accepting for himself at last the role of man and father. He marries his boyhood sweetheart Anne Stanton, to whom he had once in love and innocence committed his life irrevocably. In marrying Anne, Jack saves her in much the same way Pip saves Estella at the end of *Great Expectations*. Anne is the symbol to him of his lost innocence, and in redeeming her he at last redeems himself. Having accepted the past with its hate and love, its guilt and pride, its evil and good, Jack can be regenerated into the world of the present, redeemed through suffering and self-knowledge.

When Stark and Adam destroy each other, Jack emerges from the vicarious experience of their deaths as the synthesis of their alternatives, as a whole man. Through the responsibility his manhood imposes on him, he brings the Scholarly Attorney, old and dying, into his home. Finally, it is the old man, the religious fanatic, the "unreal" father from whom Jack learns the ultimate facts of life, who becomes a "real" father. ("Each of us is the son of a million fathers.") Jack comes to believe in the old man's religious doctrine that " 'The creation of evil is . . . the index of God's glory and His power. That had to be so that the creation of good might be the index of man's glory and power. But by God's help. By His help and His wisdom' " (p. 437)

Through his "father," Jack is able to understand the significance of Cass Mastern's life in the "eye of God." After Jack's nominal father dies and he has completed his study of Cass Mastern, fulfilling at last all of his obligations to the past, he can leave Judge Irwin's house, the womb of his rebirth, and "go into the convulsion of the world, out of history into history and the awful responsibility of time." While Cass has sacrificed his life to redeem himself, Jack achieves redemption somewhat easily and painlessly. For this reason, Jack's ultimate salvation seems externally imposed (redemption as happy ending), abstract and literary rather than real. Yet to object to Warren's fine novel because it falls short of its potentialities seems finally presumption. To have it better than it is would be at the expense of gambling with what it has already achieved—a fool's risk. All the King's Men is a great scarred bear of a book whose faults and virtues determine one another. The greatness of this bear devolves upon the magnificence of its faults and the transcendence into art of its palpable mortality.

3 · The Double Vision:

The Victim by Saul Bellow

> For no one can judge a criminal until he recognizes that he is just such a criminal as the man standing before him and that he, perhaps, is more than all men, to blame for that crime.
>
> —*The Brothers Karamazov*

1

SAUL BELLOW is a rarity among American novelists. He is not a child prodigy. I say *is* not because most of our "marvelous boys" have, in the face of time, stalwartly refused to age, have instead become elder statesmen-child prodigies, senile innocents, imaginary boys in real bull rings. Bellow was twenty-nine when his first novel, *Dangling Man* (1944), was published. At twenty-nine so many of our talented writers had already indicated their their most significant work was behind them that they had neither other voices nor other rooms, only new dust jackets for the nostalgic recreations of their earlier works. What is so remarkable about Bellow's career is that, while continuing to grow as a writer, he has risked transaction, each time out, with a different unchartered territory of the novel. In *The Victim* (1947) he has written the best of our nightmare novels. *The Adventures of Augie March* (1953), for all the diffusion of its picaresque variety of incident, is as rich and dense in experience as any novel written in our time. And *Henderson the Rain King* (1959), set in that undiscovered Africa of the spirit, is something else again—a serious comic fantasy with the pitch of insight of a major novel. It seems clear, as of 1964, that Bellow is our most valuable living novelist, an adventurous talent of extraordinary resources of vision.

Bellow's longer fiction readily divides itself into two main groups: the novels of depth, of claustrophobic internal exploration, influenced by Dostoevsky (*Dangling Man, The Victim,* and *Seize the Day*), and the novels of breadth, of sensation and experience, of physical and spiritual quest (*The Adventures of Augie March* and *Henderson the Rain King*). Inevitably, since Bellow is not two men, the preoccupations of each group reside to some extent in the other. It is somewhat unfortunate that Bellow's reputation, for good and ill, rests so heavily on *The Adventures of Augie March*, a remarkable if over extended picaresque novel with all the vices of its ambition. At its best, *Augie March* has real beauty, particularly the scenes of Augie's childhood and the portrait of Grandma Lausch; but too much of the second half of the book, in striving for a kind of grandiosity (what the New York *Times* book page calls "greatness"), seems willfully eccentric and inflated. I have chosen to deal with *The Victim* not only because it seems to me one of the important novels of our time, but because it is exemplary of the complex concerns of all of Bellow's novels. Since *Dangling Man* anticipates it, treats in less dramatic and more explicit fashion the same victim-victimizer paradox, it may be useful to move into *The Victim* by way of a brief analysis of Bellow's first novel.

The dangling man, Joseph, might be characterized as a sensitive and intelligent Robert Cohn who did not go to Princeton. This is not as patently facetious as it sounds. Bellow is so much at odds with the Hemingway code that the two form a significant polarity. In his first journal entry—the novel is written in the formal guise of a journal (notes from the nether world of uncommitment)—Joseph writes:

Today, the code of the athlete, of the tough boy . . . is stronger than ever. Do you have feelings? There are correct and incorrect ways of indicating them. Do you have an inner life? It's nobody's business but your own. Do you have emotions? Strangle them. To a degree, everyone obeys this code. And it does admit of a limited kind of candor, a close-mouthed straightforwardness. But on the truest, it has an inhibitory effect. Most serious matters are closed to the hardboiled. They are unpracticed in introspection, and therefore badly equipped to deal with opponents they cannot shoot like big game or outdo in daring.[1]

1 Saul Bellow, *The Dangling Man* (New York: Vanguard Press, 1944), p. 9. All quotations are from this edition.

Joseph's main "opponent" is himself and though ostensibly well equipped to deal with him—Joseph is *practiced* in intellection—he comes off second best; he is ultimately self-defeated.

Joseph dangles because he is denied context; he is 1-A, unemployed and unemployable, waiting to be drafted into the Second World War, in effect waiting to die. The novel chronicles Joseph's deteriorating state of soul. As his life passes in review like the movietone March of Time, Joseph reflects on its meaning, searching in vain for an existential moral code to which he can anchor his commitment. Since Joseph has nothing to do, is a kind of nonparticipant in the "real world," he can function (he thinks), if function is the word for it, as a detached observer. Detachment, however, is not easily come by. Joseph is a sufferer (like all Bellow's heroes), and detachment while others are being killed in war can only occasion feelings of guilt and impotence. Like Proust's narrator, Joseph has no real present and so must recapture the past if only to assert his existence, to justify himself to himself. The present, he tells himself hopefully, offers him a one-shot freedom, a time to come to terms with ultimates.

But his freedom, like his detachment, is illusory, another of the degrading ironies life plays on him. He discovers that there is no freedom without choice, and no choice without commitment, that while he is an isolate, his spiritual quest is a fraud: "And goodness is achieved not in a vacuum, but in the company of other men, attended by love. I, in this room, separate, alienated, distrustful, find in my purpose not an open world but a closed, hopeless jail" (p. 92). Joseph's symposiums with his imaginary alter ego, the Spirit of Alternatives (which anticipate the Leventhal-Allbee confrontations in *The Victim*), indicate the futility of the inner life divorced from the possibility of outward participation; finally, they become a kind of intellectual onanism, a further manifestation of Joseph's spiritual deterioration.

Though a man of rigorous principle, Joseph is continually betrayed by unrestrainable impulses. A partisan of nonviolence (Joseph is violently antiviolence), victimized perhaps by the ethos of war, he commits one act of violence after another. The

outer world represented by the war and its degenerative ramifications—Joseph's profiteering brother Amos, his feeble-minded
exhibitionist neighbor Vanaker, his cold-blooded intellectual
friend Abt—has become sterile and brutal, brutalizing Joseph in
its image. Joseph's aimless rages, though directed at particular
objects, are really, Bellow indicates, aimed at himself. When
his identity is denied, he asserts it by striking out in rage at the
man who has ignored him. When a Communist who knew
Joseph when he was in the party refuses to recognize him in a
restaurant, Joseph confronts the man and makes a public scene.
When his landlord turns off his heat and electricity, the af-
fronted Joseph beats him up. Joseph is saying in effect, "I beat
you, therefore you know I am, therefore I am."

The most "symbolic" of Joseph's acts of violence is his un-
authorized spanking of his barbaric teen-aged niece Etta. In a
finely rendered scene, Etta, who like her successful parents,
identifies poverty with unimportance, treats Joseph rudely,
refusing to let him listen to Haydn on *her* phonograph because
she wants to hear Cugat. That she strongly resembles Joseph
suggests that, in spanking her, Joseph is beating what he finds
detestable in himself, or rather (like Leventhal with Allbee),
is beating the objectification of himself. Etta succeeds in further victimizing Joseph by letting her parents infer that Joseph's
attack was sexual (because of their physical resemblance, a
kind of transferred onanism). Joseph, victimized further by his
own free-floating sense of guilt, is unable to deny it.

Joseph's sense of guilt, indeterminate and obsessive, haunts
him like an idiot ghost, forcing him to assume responsibility
for sins not his own. Jeff Forman, a classmate of Joseph's whose
plane was shot down in combat, provides Joseph with an objective occasion to accommodate his guilt. By not participating,
by not risking his life, Joseph had let others die for him. Forman is the personal symbol—his falling plane looms through
the novel shadowing Joseph's fall—of Joseph's culpability. A
self-conscious Dostoevskian, Joseph wants to enter the war, not
to kill but to be killed, to be purged of his guilt. Unable to
bear the terrible responsibility of his nominal freedom, he gives
himself up to the army, seeking redemption perhaps through
death, seeking escape from the consciousness of his guilt

through mindless action. Joseph writes: "Long live regimentation!" On this high-pitched irony, the novel ends.

By using the form of a journal in *Dangling Man*, Bellow avoids, one would think, the purely technical problem of structure. Though the organization of *Dangling Man* seems arbitrary—there is no apparent link between one incident and another and, consequently, no dramatic progression—it is a rigidly disciplined work. Nothing takes place in the novel that is not directly relevant to the central concern. If anything, *Dangling Man* is too tightly constructed, too sparse of novelistic flesh. Joseph, isolated from his brethren like his Biblical counterpart, has no world. Similarly, the novel exists in no real world, only a peripheral one, limited by Joseph's abortive contacts outside himself.

2

The Victim, Bellow's second novel, is traditionally plotted, well-made in the Jamesian sense. Yet even with its tightness of structure, *The Victim* has a real—a suffocatingly real—sense of life. The novel opens:

On some nights New York is as hot as Bangkok. The whole continent seems to have moved from its place and slid nearer the equator, the bitter gray Atlantic to have become green and tropical, and the people thronging the streets, barbaric fellahin among the stupendous monuments of their mystery, the lights of which, a dazing profusion, climb upward endlessly into the heat of the sky.[2]

This passage is impressive as description, evoking the oppressive humidity of a hot New York summer night, but it serves also to set an emotional atmosphere in which the victims, Leventhal and Allbee, will be seen sweltering throughout the novel, and it suggests Leventhal's spiritual malaise. Bellow follows with, "On such a night, Asa Leventhal alighted from a Third Avenue train," and we are gradually led into the anteroom of Leventhal's hothouse consciousness. By introducing Leventhal in conjunction with the suffocating heat, Bellow makes the atmosphere a reflector of Leventhal's interior suffocation.

2 Saul Bellow, *The Victim* (New York: Viking Press, Compass Books, 1956), p. 3. All quotations are from this edition.

In his way, Leventhal is also a dangling man (as Joseph is also a victim). Waiting for his wife to return from a stay with his widowed mother, he lives (like Joseph) in a state of impermanence and unreality. A dangling isolate, Leventhal is at his most vulnerable when Allbee appears, a human ruin from the darkness of Leventhal's past, to accuse him of having destroyed his life. Allbee's case is this: he had recommended Leventhal, then out of work, to his employer Rudiger; Leventhal, out of intentional malice (Allbee had once made anti-Semitic remarks in his presence), had insulted Rudiger; infuriated at Leventhal, Rudiger had fired Allbee; unable to get another job, broken by the desertion and death of his wife, Allbee had gradually degenerated to his present derelict state, for which Leventhal is mostly responsible. Allbee, whose name suggests that Bellow intends him as a kind of objective correlative for existence, or at least Leventhal's existence, assails Leventhal's self-image, and intensifies his thinly repressed sense of inadequacy. Rationally Leventhal knows that Allbee's charges are untrue, but his own comparative prosperity (for which he feels guilty) and his excruciating sensitivity to anti-Semitism make him vulnerable to Allbee's claim on him. In a sense, Allbee makes him believe what he has always believed though never admitted, that he is inadequate, that his success, small as it is, could have been achieved only by some kind of accident—some universal imbalance.

Though he vehemently denies Allbee's accusations, Leventhal feels strangely responsible for Allbee's deterioration. At one point, after he has already committed himself to Allbee, Leventhal has a flash of self-deceived insight. He wonders: "Had he unknowingly, that is unconsciously, wanted to get back at Allbee?" He then, unable to face even this possibility, denies that he had, consciously refuses all responsibility for Allbee's fall. Despite the assurance of his denial, Leventhal continues to behave toward Allbee as if he had in some interior confessional already admitted his culpability. Leventhal is not so much Allbee's victim as his own. A kind of materialized ghost from Leventhal's haunted psyche, Allbee is not the cause but the occasion of Leventhal's victimization—the objectification of his free-floating guilt.

Allbee is Leventhal's reflection, as seen in one of those freakishly distorting Coney Island mirrors: "He was taller than Leventhal but not nearly so burly; large framed but not robust," a kind of stretched-out version of Leventhal. In implication, Leventhal's meeting with Allbee, like Joseph's with his imaginary alter ego, is an existential I-thou confrontation. Allbee, as victim and accuser, not only releases Leventhal's worst and most hidden fears about himself but also embodies them. Bellow defines the nature of their relationship in their first strange meeting in the park.

On a suffocatingly, muggy night, Leventhal wanders into the park, seeking refuge from the heat. When he starts to leave he is accosted by a man who seems vaguely familiar, a deformed shadow from some dark corridor of his past. The man, Kirby Allbee, claims that he has sent Leventhal a letter, in which he makes an appointment to meet him in the park. Though he has not received Allbee's note, Leventhal has, out of a kind of psychic insight, come to the assigned spot at the assigned time, unwittingly answering Allbee's request. It is an insane confrontation. In self-righteous heat, each accuses the other of lying, yet ironically both have, from their limited knowledge, been telling the truth. Allbee insists that Leventhal is pretending not to have received his letter.

"Why should I pretend?" said Leventhal excitedly, "What reason have I got to pretend? I don't know what letter you're talking about. You haven't got anything to write me for. I haven't thought about you in years, frankly, and I don't know why you think I care whether you exist or not. What, are we related?"
"By blood? No, no . . . heavens!" Allbee laughed. [p. 29]

This is a moment, in the classic sense, of recognition. Underlying Leventhal's question, which is in impulse no less unpleasant than Allbee's answer, is the notion that his compassion has familial, or, in a sense tribal, boundaries. The anti-Semitic Allbee wants none of Leventhal's tainted blood, yet both sense— this is implicit in the exchange—that they are in some fundamental way, related. Their relatedness is what the novel is profoundly about. The two are secret sharers, though in a Dostoevskean rather than Conradian sense. Allbee is not to Leventhal, as Leggatt is to the Captain, a primordial alter ego, the personification of his evil possibilities; he is, as Smerdyakov is to Ivan (Svidrigailov to Raskolnikov), the grotesque exaggeration of his counterpart. He represents Leventhal's failings carried to their logical insanity. While we learn a great deal about Leventhal's background, we have only a nodding acquaintance with Allbee's life before he became inextricably connected with Leventhal. Allbee is somewhat of a mystery to us in the sense that human personality is never wholly explicable, in the sense that Leventhal, prior to Allbee's confrontation, has been a stranger to himself.

Though Allbee performs a symbolic role in the novel, Bellow has rendered him as real, decaying flesh and blood. As we begin to find Allbee unreclaimably depraved—a bigot and a fraud— we discover that he has, in part, been telling the truth, that the Willistons, honorable people, thought him once a fine man. Our responses are jarred; perhaps we had been wrong about him; perhaps Leventhal *is* somewhat at fault. And in the sense that a man, regardless of his intentions, is responsible for the consequences of his acts, Leventhal is partly to blame for Allbee's degeneration. In any event, we are not permitted to be *wholly* certain about anything. The truth of *The Victim* is complex, and Bellow refuses to be conclusive merely for the sake of neatness; there is always another possibility, a further ambiguity. Rather than cancel one another out as they might, Bellow's complex of awarenesses—each scene has manifold possibilities—enlarges the experience, intensifies and deepens its meaning. Allbee is Leventhal's devil, but he is also, like Leventhal, his own victim. Suffering a vague sense of responsibility for his wife's death, Allbee as a penance uses the money she has left him to destroy himself. Out of a kind of masochistic principle, yet a principle nevertheless, he refuses to profit in any way as a consequence of her death. He is then like Leventhal in that he seeks an occasion to punish himself in order to redeem his guilt. Leventhal is his occasion, as he is Leventhal's. In victimizing Leventhal, Allbee consciously degrades himself. But victimizing Leventhal is not enough; he feels compelled, since Leventhal as Jew is the enemy (his natural victim and unmerciful judge), to love him and finally to identify with him. Allbee manifests the very qualities he claims to hate in Leventhal: his self-pity, his aggressiveness, his defensiveness, his self-righteousness, his, in Allbee's anti-Semitic notion, Jewishness.

When Allbee moves into Leventhal's apartment, their identification is further intensified. Coming home after a two-day absence, Leventhal finds himself (like Golyadkin in Dostoevsky's *The Double*) locked out of his own apartment by his pretender-self. When he breaks down the door and discovers Allbee and a strange (though familiar) woman in different states of undress, he is not so much embarrassed as outraged. ("Leventhal flushed thickly, 'In my bed!'") This is a powerful and complex scene. In finding Allbee in his bed with a woman who resembles the landlady Mrs. Nunez, whom Leventhal has covertly desired, Leventhal is momentarily horrified, as if Allbee has in some way cuckolded him. Leventhal is particularly vulnerable to this humiliation. Before his marriage, when his wife had confessed to him that she was still involved in an affair with a married man, he had reacted violently, breaking off the engagement. In discovering himself locked out of his apartment, Leventhal experiences a sense of dispossession, almost as if Allbee has usurped his identity or even his very existence. Moreover, Leventhal's identification with "his double" has become so complete that as a consequence of Allbee's act, Leventhal feels guilty, as if he himself had been unfaithful to his wife. Finally, Leventhal senses that Allbee has betrayed him, that he has corrupted his bed as he has dirtied his life.

As Allbee attempts to identify with Leventhal, Leventhal, fulfilling the implied pattern of the relationship, unconsciously imitates Allbee. Though he finds drinking, in particular Allbee's chronic drunkenness, repugnant, Leventhal drinks himself into a stupor at his friend Harkavy's house. Getting drunk for Leventhal is the ultimate degradation, a way of sharing Allbee's private Hell. He becomes so committed to his victimizer-self that when Harkavy, with misguided good intention, asks the suffering Leventhal for his confidence, Leventhal is unable to betray Allbee to him. As Leventhal has learned from his previous unsuccessful attempts at communicating his problem, he is, for the time being, condemned to isolation; he must bear the burden of Allbee alone. Ironically, his victimizer, Allbee, becomes the only one with whom he can communicate.

The nature of their communication becomes, out of the similarity of their wounds, increasingly intimate. Their mutual repulsion, an objectified self-repulsion, evolves, or rather inverts, through their sense of likeness, into a grotesque attraction:

> Allbee bent forward and laid his hand on the arm of Leventhal's chair, and for a short space the two men looked at each other and Leventhal felt himself singularly drawn with a kind of affection. It oppressed him, it was repellent. He did not know what to make of it. Still, he welcomed it, too. He was remotely disturbed to see himself so changeable. However, it did not seem just then to be a serious fault. [p. 224]

This is the moment of closest connection between the two. Through the catalyst of their desperation, their hate is transformed into compassion, into something like love. Allbee, vaguely homosexual, then insists on fingering Leventhal's hair. Fascinated by his touch, Leventhal is for a time incapable of resisting, until, horrified by the implications of his reaction, he roughly pushes Allbee away. Leventhal's is less a homosexual response, though it is that too, than a deeply compassionate one; he is capable of loving even his most vicious antagonist. It is also a moment of obscene identification between the two. In experiencing attraction to his worst self, which is, in implication, the evil of the world (Hell), Leventhal is yielding to his self-degrading instincts, resolving his guilt by falling deeper into corruption. Bellow is suggesting here that ultimately the best and worst instincts of man are not always distinguishable. Heaven, which is redemption, can only and finally be reached through Hell.

At its most malicious, Allbee's persecution of Leventhal is compelled by a need to self-dramatize before an audience, to have someone, preferably his natural enemy, recognize him, understand him, and, finally, love him. In the process, Allbee succeeds in identifying with Leventhal to the extent that when Leventhal's brother Max appears, Allbee, who is an only child, finds it difficult to believe that Leventhal could have had a brother, that Leventhal's background might have been different from his. "I don't know what made me think you were an only child, like me." In a rare moment of guilelessness, Allbee impulsively confesses his loneliness: "I often used to wish there were two of us." This is a significant revelation. Having attached himself to Leventhal, Allbee has, in a sense, fulfilled his childhood wish; he has found, for a time, another of himself.

In an act of ultimate identification, Allbee attempts to kill himself, and, or more likely in his stead, Leventhal. Though Allbee only vaguely realizes this at the time, he wants to commit a kind of suicide—a transferred suicide—in which his other self, Leventhal, will die for him. When they come together several years later, Allbee tries to explain his intention to Leventhal:

> "I want you to know one thing," said Allbee. "That night . . . I wanted to put an end to myself. I wasn't thinking of hurting you. I suppose you would have been . . . but I wasn't thinking of you. You weren't even in my mind."
> Leventhal laughed outright at this.
> "You could have jumped in the river. That's a funny lie. Why tell it? Did you have to use my kitchen?"
> Allbee glanced around restlessly. The bays that rose into his loose blond hair became crimson. "No," he said miserably. "Well, anyhow, I don't remember how it was. I must have been demented. When you turn against yourself, nobody else means anything to you either." [p. 293]

Allbee, in any event, believes that he is telling the truth. He has, as we've seen, identified with Leventhal as the source and image of his degradation, and so by killing Leventhal—we are led to suspect that Allbee has no real intention of dying himself—he would be destroying the objectification of his debased self, killing himself symbolically. Before they part, Allbee acknowledges his indebtedness to Leventhal ("'I know I owe you something'"). However, Allbee is unable to articulate just what that "something" is. It is the final consequence of their shared identity; in saving his own life, Leventhal saves Allbee's.

As Leventhal makes possible Allbee's physical rehabilitation, Allbee makes possible Leventhal's redemption. At the start of the novel, Leventhal, isolated from himself, can have no real connection with others. By victimizing him, Allbee breaks down Leventhal's self-limiting defenses, destroys him in effect into wholeness. His confrontation with Allbee, which has all the aspects of a nightmare, operates for Leventhal as a spiritual shock treatment. Spiritually ill, Leventhal can achieve salvation only after he has come to terms with the lower depths of his being—his Allbee. His spiritual descent is an illustration of the Heraclitean paradox, that the way up and the way down are one and the same. Leventhal is on the verge of being physically destroyed—the correlative of his moral degeneration—when he is wakened from a fitful, despondent sleep by the gas perfumes (Leventhal associates it with the scent of Allbee's woman) Allbee has jetted from an unlighted stove. Leventhal instinctively acts to save his life, and in almost ritual progression, he chases Allbee out of his house (exorcising his devil), shuts off the gas, and opens the windows: the cold air revives him. Purged of his guilt and his hate, Leventhal (like the hero of Salinger's "For Esmé—with Love and Squalor") is able at last to sleep undisturbed in the grace of his redemption.

The last chapter, which serves as an epilogue and gloss to the experience of the novel is somewhat unsatisfying. What is wrong is not that it is inconclusive—no finally serious novel can be conclusive—but that it seems, for the most part, unnecessary. Several years after the main action has taken place, Leventhal and Allbee accidentally meet again in the lobby of a Broadway theatre. As if in justification of Allbee's thesis that a man has infinite possibilities for changing his life (" 'It makes sense to me that a man can be born again' "), both Leventhal and Allbee have ameliorated, if not their lives, at least their situations. Though only moderately prosperous, Leventhal has a better job, has relocated to a better neighborhood, and, as Bellow insists on telling us, no longer feels that "he had got away with it." Though they had been married for some time before his wife Mary's prolonged visit to her mother, Leventhal is about to become a father for the first time. (His potency, Bellow suggests, is a consequence of his redemption.) For the most part, Leventhal's change, though genuine, is hardly noticeable, while Allbee's transformation is ostentatious, yet, as we discover on closer inspection, illusory. The inversion is ironic though somewhat easy. Leventhal, as real man, has through his redemption undergone a real change, while Allbee, the patina of a man, has achieved a factitious rebirth, a rebirth made possible by some kind of interior death.

The subplot, if it may properly be called that, which deals

with Leventhal's brother Max's family, is contrapuntal to the main situation. Leventhal's reactions to his brother's family parallel and illuminate his behavior toward Allbee; the two separate and distinct contexts enable us to cross-check the validity of Leventhal's perceptions in each. With Max prospecting in Texas for a job and a place to settle, Leventhal feels responsible for his brother's wife and children, who live in depressed conditions in that oddly isolated section of New York City, Staten Island, and somewhat guilty for what seems to him Max's desertion of them. At the outset of the novel, Leventhal learns that his youngest nephew, Mickey, is sick and he leaves work during a rush period, initiating one guilt to propitiate another, to help his sister-in-law Elena. The ferry ride to Staten Island, which carries with it echoes of the mythic voyage across the river Styx into hell, operates in the novel as one of the physical manifestations of Leventhal's spiritual descent:

> There was a slow heave about the painted and rusted hulls in the harbor. The rain had gone out to the horizon, a dark band far overreaching the faint marks of the shore. On the water the air was cooler, but on the Staten Island side the green tarnished sheds were sweltering, the acres of cement widely spattered with sunlight. The disembarking crowd spread through them, going toward the line of busses that waited at the curb with threshing motors, in a shimmer of fumes. [p. 6]

The physical properties of Leventhal's outer world are always, in some form, manifestations of his inner disturbances—a paranoid's dream world.

At first Leventhal is unable to cope with Elena's old-world superstitions, but he finally persuades her to send Mickey, who has been running a high temperature, to a hospital so that he can be given the care he obviously needs. When Mickey dies in the hospital—it happens just when Leventhal feels himself inextricably trapped by Allbee's accusations—he suffers pangs of guilt as if by insisting on the hospital he has murdered the child. He senses in his confusion that Allbee's accusations are somehow justified in Mickey's death. The objects of his guilt proliferate. His guilt feelings toward Allbee are transferred to Elena who, he is willing to believe, holds him responsible for the death of his nephew. His sense of guilt for his brother's apparent failure as a father and his own failure to save Mickey is transferred in part to Allbee, one implementing and intensifying the other until Leventhal's guilt becomes objectless, all inclusive, unbearable. He drinks himself into oblivion immediately after he hears of Mickey's death, an act for him of moral suicide, an emulation (as penance) of Allbee's self-destructive pattern. Since Elena is not Jewish, Leventhal is particularly vulnerable to her opinions of him. Somewhere in the ether of his consciousness he disapproves of his brother's union, vaguely attributing a mixed marriage to a failure of principle on both sides. Yet, aware of his own inadequacy, and seeing it mirrored in his brother's apparent escape from family responsibilities, he senses that the failure is essentially on his side—his. Consequently, he resents what he imagines is Elena's (and more intensely her old-world mother's) right to disapprove of him. As in his relationship with Allbee, Leventhal feels persecuted because he believes he should be persecuted.

Haunted by the recollections of his mother's madness and the specter of his own potential, Leventhal thinks he sees his mother's tendencies manifested in Elena. Part of Leventhal's terrible sense of loss at Mickey's death comes from his covert identification with him; they are both victims, in a sense, of their mothers' insanity. Insanity, for Leventhal, is the nature of the destroyer, *is* the destroyer. When Allbee first confronts him with his accusations, Leventhal suspects him, though not without cause, of being demented. Out of his own chaos, Leventhal espies madness at every turn—Allbee, Rudiger, Elena, her mother—obsessively attributing to others his darkest fears about himself. However, Leventhal's world is, even from an objective point of view, somewhat insane. Therefore, within his distorted vision, a projecting into others his own deceived sense of himself, his perceptions are in part accurate. At the start of the novel he is somewhat aware of his tendency to misconceive in terms of his own preoccupations. For example, in his first view of Elena,

He observed that her eyes were anxious, altogether too bright and too liquid; there was a superfluous energy in her movements, a suggestion of distraction or even of madness not very securely held in check. But he was too susceptible to such suggestions. He was aware of that, and he warned himself not to be hasty. [p. 7]

Though he overstates Elena's disturbance, which is temporary hysteria, not insanity, Leventhal has enough control at this point to be aware of the limited reliability of his view. Yet for all Leventhal's awareness of his "susceptibility," under the combined pressures of Allbee's persecution and Mickey's illness and death, his rational monitor breaks down; his vision becomes distorted. Unable to distinguish the external world from his obsessive internal one, he loses almost all sense of reality and his perceptions become in effect insane.

Much of the impact of *The Victim* resides in Bellow's ability to keep the reader's point of view limited to Leventhal's, making the reader a sympathetic participant in his nightmare experience. At Mickey's funeral, Leventhal is horrified at what he is sure must be Elena's reaction to him:

He gazed at Max's burly back and his sunburnt neck, and, as his glance moved across the polished rows of benches, he saw Elena sitting between Villani and a priest. The look she gave him was one of bitter anger. Though the light was poor, there was no mistaking it. Her face was white and straining. "What've I done?" he thought; his panic was as great as if he had never foreseen this. He was afraid to let her catch his eye and did not return her look. . . . What would he do if then and there—imagining the worst—she began to scream at him, accusing him? Once more she turned her face to him over her shoulder; it seemed to be blazing in its whiteness. She must be mad. [p. 182]

This is at once a powerful, realistic scene and an halucinatory vision not unworthy of Kafka. Nevertheless, that Elena hates Leventhal at this time seems, given the picture we have had of Elena through Leventhal's eyes, more than possible. Nor can we easily dismiss Leventhal's suspicion of her madness—that too seems possible, even probable. We allow for a certain amount of exaggeration in Leventhal's perceptions, but they are, after all, the only ones we have to rely on. However, when we discover through Max's testimony that Leventhal has completely misread Elena's look, that if anything she is grateful to him rather than antipathetic, that she is not by any reasonable standard insane, we are jarred into re-evaluating the import of Leventhal's entire experience. Yet the possibility remains, though it is a slight one, that Max also may be mistaken. Bellow makes the problem of distinguishing appearance from reality, of affixing moral responsibility for particular and universal wrongs, seem all but prohibitively complex. Each discovery that Bellow permits us to make takes us farther away from a pure and simple answer, yet nearer to the final discovery that there is no discoverable final truth, only a profound and ambiguous approximation of it.

Caught up in a cycle of guilt and persecution, as Leventhal becomes more obsessed with being persecuted he becomes correspondingly more guilt-ridden. Leventhal's behavior toward his former employer and friend Williston curiously parallels Allbee's toward Leventhal. Believing out of a sense of persecution that the uncommitted Williston is sympathetic to Allbee, Leventhal goes to his home and irrationally accuses his friend of having done him an injury. Leventhal's accusations, like Allbee's of him, are vague insinuations, implying a conspiratorial awareness on the part of his hallucined betrayer. Provoked by Leventhal's badgering, Williston satisfies Leventhal's ambivalent quest for absolution and punishment, and admits that he considers Leventhal in part responsible for Allbee's loss of his job. In response, Leventhal asserts, imitating Allbee's manner of defensive attack, that Williston's position is only a more genteel version of Allbee's, that Williston, underneath his platitudinous liberalism, is also anti-Semitic. Defensive, Williston insists that he does not think that Leventhal actually *intended* to hurt Allbee, though it is an admissible possibility, but whatever his intentions the effect was the same; Rudiger fired Allbee because of Leventhal (which is another of their double correspondences). Though the explanations Leventhal wrests from Williston are painful to him, he compulsively provokes them, a fascinated spectator at his own execution. " 'So . . .' Leventhal said blankly, 'In a way it really seems to be my fault, doesn't it?' He paused and gazed abstractly at Williston, his hands still motionless at his knees" (p. 117). Though Leventhal has a moment before accused Williston of prejudice, he readily accepts Williston's verdict. This is Leventhal's first explicit admission of blame for Allbee's comedown, though he had implicitly accepted it all along. However, his *conscious* acceptance of responsibility is a moral act that makes possible his ultimate redemption.

This leads us to the central moral dilemma of the novel: How

far can a man be held responsible for the unintentional consequences of his acts? Bellow never wholly resolves the question,
but he suggests that the intention and the act are not ethically
separable, that morality relies on each man's existential responsibility for his acts. Yet Bellow is aware that absolute responsibility is an impossible ideal, a saint's ideal, and that, in a
practical, moral sense, an intentional evil is more egregious than
an unconscious one. Though Leventhal assures himself that he
had not insulted Rudiger to get back at Allbee, he is nevertheless disturbed because he suspects that Williston has not believed him; his persecution, as always, extends beyond his
culpability.

What Allbee and Leventhal share most is the feeling that
the dark forces that control civilization are for one reason or
another persecuting them. A New Englander with aristocratic
pretensions, Allbee equates New Yorkers with the "children of
Caliban" (Jews of a kind), who have persecuted him by driving
out the light as "Moses punished the Egyptians with darkness."
Ironically, Allbee is in a sense more Jewish than Leventhal.
His anti-Semitic obsessions have made him more profoundly
involved with Jewish tradition and more knowledgeable about
Judaism itself than his Jewish enemy. If Allbee's is the guilt of
the persecutor, then in some essential way the persecutor and
persecuted are one. The Jew and Jew-hater, as close as opposing
magnetic poles, become, in their mutual isolation and self-hate,
interchangeable—indistinguishable.

Leventhal, a victim of real and imaginary persecution, feels
guilty because he believes that his suffering, like all suffering,
is deserved, yet he cannot recognize his own mortal sin. At the
same time he suspects that civilization, alien to the Jew, is a
manifestation of a universal conspiracy, malevolent and unseen,
determined on persecuting the outsider—Leventhal. Throughout
the novel, Leventhal, as if rolling the stone of Sisyphus, seeks to
find out if there is a black list in his profession, some vague
conspiracy that performs in microcosm the Great Work of Universal Injustice. At various times it seems to him that he has
uncovered the consiracy in action, with its hand in the till, so
to speak, though he is never able to confirm his suspicions.

At their final meeting, the "successful" Allbee tells Leventhal that he has "made his peace with whoever runs things." In other words, Allbee has sacrificed his vestigial sense of self to survive in a world he had, though unknowingly, made. The irony is that he has "made his peace" not with the real world but with his own paranoiac version of it. As Allbee leaves, Leventhal, unrestrainedly curious, calls after him: " 'Wait a minute, what's your idea who runs things?' " Allbee has already gone; Leventhal never gets an answer. "Who runs things" is the final insoluble mystery.

If Allbee is Leventhal's antagonist, and double, he is also Leventhal's savior, the unwitting means to his redemption. A similar ritual process takes place for Tommy Wilhelm in *Seize the Day* and Henderson in *Henderson the Rain King*. Allbee, like Tamkin, like Dahfu, is a kind of fraud-saint, a redeemer in spite of himself. All of Bellow's novels, with the possible exception of *The Adventures of Augie March*, deal with the sufferer, the seismographic recorder of world guilt who, confronted by a guilt-distorted correlative of himself, seeks within the bounds of his own hell the means to his heaven. Leventhal is redeemed through succumbing to the temptations of his devil; he crosses the threshold of hell, descends to its deepest parts and, heroically, for Leventhal is finally a hero, comes back again, better if not greatly wiser.

3

The best of our novelists seem to achieve one transcendent performance, followed by self-imitation, or loss of energy, or the substitution of will for creation. Wright Morris is an exception; Saul Bellow is another. Though less prolific than Morris, Bellow has a greater range of concerns and is, on the whole, a more profound if less uncompromisingly difficult a novelist. In an essay in *Esquire*, characteristically entitled "No! in Thunder," Leslie Fiedler, one of Bellow's earliest admirers, admonishes Bellow for resolving *Henderson the Rain King* affirmatively, because (and I am somewhat oversimplifying Fiedler's position) the only honest response to the contemporary world is denial. Though Fiedler's construction is not wholly unreasonable, he argues it too literally (as Stevens tells us, "After the final no there comes a yes") and applies it speciously as if it were an esthetic principle. Moreover, in making his point, Fiedler misreads, or rather narrowly reads, the ending of Bellow's novel. What is being affirmed in Henderson's ecstatic run across the Newfoundland ice? Contemporary civilization? The universe? Hardly. The regeneration of the self, the endurance of the spirit? In part. It is Henderson, however, not Bellow, who is euphoric; it is Henderson who is celebrating his survival, who is affirming the regeneration of his life. It is rather late in the day to be confusing a first-person protagonist with his author, but that, in effect, is what Fiedler has done. In other parts of the novel, Henderson experiences a similar euphoria (he is chronically manic), an hallucinatory sense of well-being, only to discover afterward that he has beguiled himself. The ending is at least in part ironic; otherwise why have Henderson's affirmation of life take place on a lifeless wasteland? One might answer, of course, because it happens in Newfoundland. But isn't that just the point of Bellow's irony? The new-found land is desolate; Henderson's new-found self is also somewhat illusory. Here, as throughout the novel, Henderson is quixotic. Bellow is not, however, wholly undercutting his hero. The scene is not *just* ironic as it is not just affirmative. Henderson's survival of his adventures in that treacherous dream Africa of the spirit, with all his extraordinary powers of strength and energy undiminished by the bruises of time, is in itself remarkable. As always, Henderson reasons with his feelings, not his brain, and it is his energy—the source of his life—not his self-knowledge, that he is celebrating. Henderson's ecstatic self-affirmation, "running—leaping, leaping, pounding, and tingling over the pure white lining of the gray arctic silence," is possible only where there is no real world about to deny it—where there is nothing crucial at stake to expose his well-meaning ineptitude. That Henderson, in spite of all evidence to the contrary, retains his blind illusions is his absurdity as well as his redeeming grace.

Where Bellow's first two novels are somewhat indebted to Dostoevsky and Kafka, *Henderson the Rain King* is a unique and adventurous work. It is also a conspicuously American book in the great tradition of the romance novel from Hawthorne and Melville through Faulkner. After Faulkner, Bellow is our major novelist, and his achievement (with Faulkner's) has provided seed for what appears to be one of the strongest crops of fiction in our history. The confrontation of Leventhal with Allbee, of man with his own distorted image, his fallen self, and the consequent recognition of an apparently boundless guilt, for which he suffers and for which he achieves through suffering the possibility, or illusion, of redemption, has become in various disguises one of the abiding concerns of the contemporary American novel and one of the profound moral myths of these anguished, bomb-haunted times.

4 · The Saint as a Young Man:

The Catcher in the Rye by J. D. Salinger

> There isn't anyone *any*where that isn't Sey-
> mour's Fat Lady. Don't you know that? . . .
> and don't you know—listen to me now—
> *don't you know who that Fat Lady really is?*
> . . . Ah, buddy. Ah, buddy. It's Christ Him-
> self. Christ Himself, buddy.
> —*Franny and Zooey*

IN REACTION to its long period of over-repute, J. D. Salinger's
first and only novel, *The Catcher in the Rye* (1951), has undergone in recent years a steady if overinsistent devaluation. The
more it becomes academically respectable, the more it becomes
fair game for those critics who are sworn to expose every manifestation of what seems to them a chronic disparity between
appearance and reality. It is critical child's play to find fault
with Salinger's novel. Anyone can see that the prose is
mannered (which is the pejorative word for stylized); no one
actually talks like its first-person hero Holden Caulfield. Moreover, we are told that Holden as poor little rich boy is too
precocious and specialized an adolescent for his plight to have
larger-than-prep-school significance. The novel is sentimental, it
loads the deck for Holden and against the adult world; the
small but corrupt group that Holden encounters is not a representative enough sampling to permit Salinger his inclusive judgments of the species. Holden's relation to his family is not
explored; we meet his sister Phoebe, who is a younger version of
himself, but his father never appears and his mother exists in
the novel only as a voice from a dark room; and finally, what
is Holden (or Salinger) protesting but the ineluctability of growing up, of having to assume the prerogatives and responsibilities
of manhood?

I hope I have fairly entered all of the objections to the novel,
because I think that despite them *The Catcher in the Rye* will
endure. It will endure mainly because it has life and secondly

because it is an original work full of insights into at least the particular truth of Holden's existence. Given the limited terms of its vision, Salinger's small book is almost perfectly achieved. It is, if such a distinction is meaningful, an important minor novel.

Like all of Salinger's fiction, *The Catcher in the Rye* is not only *about* innocence, it is actively *for* innocence, as if retaining one's childness were an existential possibility. The metaphor of the title—Holden's fantasy vision of standing in front of a cliff and protecting playing children from falling (Falling)—is, despite the impossibility of its realization, the only positive action affirmed in the novel. It is, in Salinger's Manichean universe of child angels and adult "phonies," the only moral alternative; otherwise all is corruption. And since to prevent the Fall is a spiritual as well as physical impossibility, Salinger's idealistic heroes are doomed to either suicide (Seymour) or insanity (Holden, Sergeant X) or mysticism (Franny); or to moral dissolution (Eloise, D. B., Mr. Antolini)—the way of the world. In Salinger's finely honed prose, at once idiomatically real and poetically stylized, we get the terms of Holden's ideal adult occupation.

Anyway, I kept picturing all these little kids playing some game in this big field of rye and all. Thousands of little kids, and nobody's around—nobody big, I mean—except me. And I'm standing on the edge of some crazy cliff. What I have to do, I have to catch everybody if they start to go over the cliff—I mean if they're running and they don't look where they're going. I have to come out from somewhere and *catch* them. That's all I'd do all day. I'd just be the catcher in the rye and all. I know it's crazy, but that's the only thing I'd really like to be.[1]

Apparently Holden's wish is purely selfless. What he wants, in effect, is to be a saint—the protector and savior of innocence. But what he also wants—for he is still one of the running children himself—is that someone prevent *his* fall. This is his paradox; he must leave innocence to protect innocence. At sixteen he is ready to shed his innocence and move like Adam into the fallen adult world, but he resists because those who

---

[1] J. D. Salinger, *The Catcher in the Rye* (New York: New American Library, 1953), p. 156. All quotations are from this edition.

are no longer innocent seem to him foolish as well as corrupt. In a sense, then, he is looking for an exemplar, a wise and good father whose example will justify his own initiation into manhood. Before Holden can become a catcher in the rye, he must find another catcher in the rye to show him how it is done.

Immediately after Holden announces his "crazy" ambition to Phoebe, he calls up an old school teacher of his, a Mr. Antolini, who is both intelligent and kind—a potential catcher in the rye.

> He was the one that finally picked up that boy that jumped out of the window. . . . James Castle. Old Mr. Antolini felt his pulse and all, and then he took off his coat and put it over James Castle and carried him all the way to the infirmary. [p. 157]

Though Mr. Antolini is sympathetic because "he didn't even give a damn if his coat got all bloody," the incident is symbolic of the teacher's failure as a catcher in the rye. For all his good intentions, he was unable to catch James Castle or prevent his fall; he could only pick him up afterward when the boy was dead. The episode of the suicide is one of the looming shadows that darkens Holden's world, and Holden seeks out Antolini because he hopes that the gentle teacher—the substitute father —will "pick him up" before he is irrevocably fallen. Holden's real quest throughout the novel is for a spiritual father (an innocent adult). When he calls Antolini all the other fathers of his world have already failed him, including his real father, whose existence in the novel is represented solely by Phoebe's childish reiteration of "Daddy's going to kill you." The fathers in Salinger's child's-eye world do not catch falling boys, boys who have been thrown out of prep school, but "kill" them. Antolini, then, represents Holden's last chance to find a catcher-father. But Antolini's inability to save Holden has been prophesied in his failure to save James Castle; the episode of Castle's death narrated earlier in the novel provides an anticipatory parallel to Antolini's unwitting destruction of Holden.

The revelation that Antolini's kindness to Holden is motivated in part by a homosexual interest, though it comes as a shock to Holden, does not wholly surprise the reader. Many of the biographical details that Salinger has told us about him through Holden predicate this possibility. For example, that he has an older and unattractive wife whom he makes a great show of kissing in public is highly suggestive; yet the discovery itself, when Holden wakes to find Antolini sitting beside him and caressing his head, has considerable impact. We experience a kind of shock of recognition, the more intense for its having been anticipated. The scene has further power because Antolini is, for the most part, a good man, and his interest in Holden is genuine as well as perverted. His advice to Holden, which is offered as from father to son, is apparently well intentioned. Though for the most part his recommendations are cleverly articulated platitudes, Antolini evinces a prophetic insight when he tells Holden, " 'I have a feeling that you're riding for some kind of a terrible, terrible fall,' " though one suspects he is, at least in part, talking about himself. Ironically, Antolini becomes the agent of his "terrible, terrible fall" by violating Holden's image of him, by becoming a false father. Having lost his respect for Antolini as a man, Holden rejects him as authority; as far as Holden is concerned Antolini's example denies the import of his words. His disillusionment with Antolini, the man who had seemed to be the wise-good father, coming as the last and most intense in a long line of disillusionments, is the final straw. To Holden it is the equivalent of the loss of God. The world, devoid of good fathers (authorities), becomes for him a soul-destroying chaos in which his survival is possible only through withdrawal into childhood, into fantasy, into psychosis.

The action of the novel is compressed into two days in which Holden discovers through a series of disillusioning experiences that the adult world is unreclaimably corrupt. At the start of the novel we learn from Holden that he has flunked out of Pencey Prep for not applying himself; he has been resistant to what he considers foolish or "phony" authority. Like almost all of Salinger's protagonists, Holden is clearly superior to his surroundings; he functions by dint of his pure sight, his innocence and sensibility, as initiate in and conscience of the world of the novel. So, allowing for the exaggerations of innocence, we can generally accept Holden's value judgments of people and places as the judgments of the novel. For example, when Holden observes his seventy-year-old, grippe-ridden history teacher picking his nose: "He made out like he was only pinching it, but he was really getting the old thumb right in there. . . . I didn't *care*, except that it's pretty disgusting to watch somebody pick their nose" (p. 12), he is not being gratuitously malicious; he is being innocent. Whereas the adult observer, no matter how scrupulous, censors his irreverent or unpleasant responses because he is ashamed of them, the child tells all. In effect, Holden is passing what amounts to a moral judgment, although he is consciously doing no more than describing his reactions. Like Jane Austen, Salinger treats fools, especially pretentious ones, mercilessly. Though Spencer may be seventy-years-old and for that alone worthy of respect, he is nevertheless platitudinous and self-indulgent, interested less in Holden than in pontificating before a captive audience. In a world in which the child is the spiritual father of the man, old age represents not wisdom but spiritual blindness and physical corruption. Spencer is not only foolish and "phony" ("Life *is* a game, boy") but in his self-righteous way also actively malicious. Though Holden's is ostensibly a social visit, the old man badgers the boy about having failed history ("'I flunked you in history because you knew absolutely nothing.'"), and then insists on reading aloud Holden's inadequate exam. In this confrontation between Holden and Spencer, there is an ironic inversion of the traditional student-teacher, son-father relationship which extends throughout the novel and throughout Salinger's fictional world. While Spencer insensitively embarrasses the already wounded Holden, who has been irrevocably expelled from Pencey, out of a childish need for personal justification, the boy is in turn mature enough to be kind to his vulnerable antagonist. Holden accepts the full burden of responsibility for his scholastic failure so as to relieve the teacher of his sense of guilt ("I told him I would've done exactly the same thing if I'd been in his place"). In compassionately protecting his teacher's feelings, Holden is in a sense performing the role of wise father; he is here a kind of catcher in the rye for a clumsy old child. Holden's compassion is extensive enough to include even those he dislikes, even those who have hurt him. As he tells Antolini later in the novel:

You're wrong about that hating business. . . . What I may do, I may hate them for a *little* while, like this guy Stradlater I knew at Pencey, and this other boy, Robert Ackley. I hated *them* once in a while—I admit it—but it doesn't last too long, is what I mean. After a while, if I didn't see them, if they didn't come in the room . . . I sort of missed them. [pp. 168–69]

As Antolini and Spencer are too corrupt to notice, Holden is unable to cope with the world, not because he hates but because he loves and the world hates.

Spencer symbolizes (which is not to say that he does not also have a particular existence) all of the stupid and destructive teacher-fathers at Pencey Prep, which is in microcosm all schools—the world. In the short scene between Holden and Spencer, Salinger evokes a sense of Holden's entire "student" experience, in which flunking out is an act of moral will rather than a failure of application. Here as throughout the novel, the wise son resists the initiatory knowledge of the false ("phony") father and retains, at the price of dispossession, his innocence. As I mentioned before, Holden is not so much rebelling against all authority or even false authority as he is searching for a just father. That there are no good fathers in the world is its and Holden's tragedy. It is the tragedy of Salinger's cosmos that the loss of innocence is irremediable. Ejected from the fallow womb of the prep school, Holden goes out alone into the world of New York City in search of some kind of sustenance. His comic misadventures in the city, which lead to his ultimate disillusion and despair—after the Antolini episode Holden wants to withdraw from the world and become a deaf-mute—make up the central action of the novel.

Holden not only suffers as a victim from the effects of the evil in this world but *for* it as its conscience, so that his experiences are exemplary. In this sense, *The Catcher in the Rye* is a religious, or, to be more exact, spiritual novel. Holden is Prince Mishkin as a sophisticated New York adolescent, and like Mishkin, he experiences the guilt, the unhappiness, and the spiritual deformities of others more intensely than he does his own misfortunes. This is not to say that Holden is without faults; he is, on occasion, silly, irritating, thoughtless, irresponsible—he has the excesses of innocence. Yet he is, as nearly as possible, without sin. The most memorable love affair Holden has experienced has had its fruition in daily checker games with

Jane Gallagher, an unhappy, sensitive girl who was his neighbor one summer. She has become the symbol to him of romantic love—that is, innocent love. When Holden discovers that his "sexy" roommate Stradlater has a date with her, he is concerned not only about the possible loss of Jane's innocence but about the loss of his dream of her, the loss of their combined checker-playing, love-innocence. Holden had one previous emotional breakdown at thirteen when his saint-brother Allie [2] died of leukemia. Allie's death is Holden's first recognition of the fact of evil—of what appears to be the gratuitous malevolence of the universe. Allie, who was, Holden tells us, more intelligent and nicer than anyone else, becomes for Holden a kind of saint-ideal. Therefore, Stradlater's rejection of an English theme on Allie's baseball glove that Holden has written for him, combined with his implication that he has "given Jane Gallagher the time," spiritually maims Holden; assails his only defense, his belief in the possibility of good in the world. ("I felt so lonesome, all of a sudden. I almost wished I was dead" [p. 46]).

It is in this state of near-suicidal despair that Holden leaves for New York. That Stradlater may have had sexual relations with Jane—the destruction of innocence is an act of irremediable evil in Holden's world—impels Holden's immediate flight from Pencey (not before he quixotically challenges the muscular Stradlater, who in turn bloodies his nose). At various times in New York Holden is on the verge of phoning Jane and twice he actually dials her number; that he is unable to reach her is symbolic of his loss of her innocence. The sexually experienced Stradlater, who is one of Holden's destructive fathers in the novel, has irreparably destroyed not so much Jane's innocence as Holden's idealized notion of her.[3] ·

In obliquely searching for good in the adult world, or at least something to mitigate his despair, Holden is continually con-

2 Holden's relation to Allie is, though less intense, the equivalent of Buddy's to Seymour in the several Glass family stories.

3 Another destructive father is Ackley, who refuses Holden solace after Holden has been morally and physically beaten by Stradlater. (The father concern is an intentional one on Salinger's part.) Both Ackley and Stradlater are two years old than Holden, and at one point Ackley reproves Holden's lack of respect, telling him, " 'I am old enough to be your father.' "

fronted with the absence of good. On his arrival in the city, he is disturbed because his cab-driver is corrupt and unsociable and, worst of all, unable to answer one of his obsessive questions, which is where the ducks in Central Park go when the lake freezes over. What Holden really wants to know is whether there is a benevolent authority that takes care of ducks. If there is one for ducks, it sensibly follows that there may be one for people as well. Holden's quest for a wise and benevolent authority, then, is essentially a search for a God principle. However, none of the adults in Holden's world have any true answers for him. When he checks into a hotel room, he is depressed by the fact that the bellboy is an old man. As sensitized recorder of the moral vibrations of his world, Holden suffers the indignity of the aged bellhop's situation for him, as he had suffered for Spencer's guilt and Ackley's self-loathing. Yet, and this is part of his tragedy, he is an impotent saint—he is unable to redeem the fallen or prevent their fall.

Where the world of Holden's school was a muted purgatory, the world of his New York hotel is an insistent Hell. From his room with a view that looks into other hotel rooms, he sees a man dress himself in women's clothes and in another room a man and woman who squirt water at each other from their mouths; this is the "real" world with its respectable shade lifted. Holden is fascinated and, in a sense, seduced by its prurience. Having lost the sense of his innocence, he seeks sexual initiation as a means of redemption. That he is generally attracted to older women suggests that his quest for a woman is really a search for a mother whose love will provide a protection against the corrupt world as well as initiate him into it. Where the father-quest is a quest for wisdom and spirit (God), the mother-quest is not ultimately for sex but for love. They are, then, different manifestations, one intellectual, the other physical, of the same spiritual quest. Holden's search for sexual experience is, Salinger indicates, the only love alternative left him after his loss of Jane. Once the possibility of innocent love ceases to exist, sexual love seems the next best thing, a necessary compensation for the loss of the first. However, Holden is only mildly disappointed when he is unable to arrange a date with a reputedly promiscuous girl whose number he has inherited from a Princeton acquaintance. For all his avowed "sexiness," he is an innocent, and his innocence-impelled fear dampens his desire. Though the women he meets are by and large less disappointing than the men, they too fail Holden and intensify his despair. That they are not as good as he would like them to be seems to him *his* fault, *his* responsibility, *his* failure.

If Jane represents sacred love profaned, the prostitute who comes to Holden's room represents profane love unprofaned. Though he agrees to have her come to his room, he refuses to make love to her once she is there. The scene is a crucial one in defining Holden's nontraditional sainthood. Not on moral principle does Holden refuse the prostitute, but because the condition of her existence—she is about Holden's age and a kind of lost innocent—depresses him. When he hangs up her dress for her he imagines

her going in a store and buying it, and nobody in the store knowing she was a prostitute. The salesman probably just thought she was a regular girl when she bought it. It made me feel sad as hell. [p. 88]

Holden suffers the girl's sadness as if her degradation were also in some way his. He would save her if he could but she is far too fallen for any catcher in the rye. But as child-saint, Holden is quixotic. In not sleeping with her he means to protect her innocence, not his own; he is spiritually, and consequently physically, unable to be a party to her further degradation. The consequences are ironic. Holden as saint refuses to victimize the prostitute, but he, in turn, is victimized by the girl and her accomplice Maurice. Though Holden has paid the girl without using her, Maurice beats Holden and extorts five extra dollars from him. This episode is a more intense recapitulation of the Stradlater experience. In both cases Holden is punished for his innocence. If the hotel is a symbolic Hell, Maurice, as far as Holden is concerned, is its chief devil. In offering Holden the girl and then humiliating him for not accepting his expensive gift, Maurice is another of Holden's evil fathers.

Like so many heroes of contemporary fiction—Morris' Boyd, Ellison's Invisible Man, Malamud's Frank, Salinger's Seymour —Holden is, for all his good intentions, an impotent savior, a butter-fingered catcher in the rye. Because he can neither save his evil world nor live in it as it is, he retreats into fantasy, into childhood. I think the end of the novel has been generally misinterpreted because of a too literal reading of Holden's divulgence in the beginning that he is telling the story from some kind of rest home. Holden is always less insane than his world. The last scene, in which Holden, watching his kid sister Phoebe go around on a merry-go-round, sits in the pouring rain suffused with happiness, is not indicative of his crack-up, as has been assumed, but of his redemption. Whereas all of the adults in his world fail him, and he, in consequence, fails them, a ten-year-old girl, whom he protects as catcher in the rye, saves him —becomes his catcher. Love is the redemptive grace. Phoebe thus replaces Jane, whose loss had initiated Holden's despair, flight, and quest for experience as salvation. Holden's pure communion with Phoebe may be construed as a reversion to childhood innocence, but this, in Salinger's world, is the only way to redemption; there is no other good. Innocence is all. Love is innocence.

After his disillusionment with Antolini, who is, in effect, the most destructive of Holden's fathers because he is apparently the most benevolent, Holden suffers his emotional breakdown. His flight from Antolini's house, like his previous flights from school and from the hotel, is an attempt at escaping evil. The three are parallel experiences except that Holden is less sure of the justness of his third flight; he wonders if he has not misjudged his otherwise sympathetic teacher: "Maybe he *was* only patting my head just for the hell of it. The more I thought about it, though, the more depressed and screwed up I got" (p. 176). The ambivalence of his response racks him. If he has misjudged Antolini, Holden has not only wronged him but wronged himself; it is he, not Antolini, who has been guilty of corruption. Consequently, he suffers both for Antolini and himself. Holden's guilt-ridden despair manifests itself in nausea and in an intense sense of physical ill-being, as if he carried the whole awful corruption of the city inside him. Walking aimlessly through the city at Christmastime, Holden experiences "the terrible, terrible fall" that Antolini had phophesied for **him:**

Every time I came to the end of a block and stepped off the goddam curb, I had this feeling that I'd never get to the other side of the street. I thought I'd go down, down, down, and nobody'd ever see me again. Boy, did it scare me. . . . Everytime I'd get to the end of the block, I'd make believe I was talking to my brother, Allie. I'd say to him, "Allie, don't let me disappear. Allie, don't let me disappear. Please, Allie." And then when I reached the other side of the street without disappearing, I'd *thank* him. [p. 178]

Like Franny's prayer to Jesus in one of Salinger's later stories, Holden's prayer to Allie is not so much an act of anguish as an act of love, though it is in part both. Trapped in an interior hell, Holden seeks redemption, not by formal appeal to God or Jesus, who have in the Christmas season been falsified and commercialized, but by praying to his saint-brother, who in his goodness had God in him.

Unable to save himself or others, Holden decides to withdraw from the world, to become a deaf-mute and live by himself in an isolated cabin, to commit a symbolic suicide. It is an unrealizable fantasy but a death wish nevertheless. However, Holden's social conscience forces him out of spiritual retirement. When he discovers an obscenity scrawled on a wall in Phoebe's school, he rubs it out with his hand to protect the innocence of the children. He is for the moment a successful catcher in the rye. But then he discovers another such notice which has been imprinted with a knife, and then another. He realizes that he cannot possibly erase all the scribbled obscenities in the world, that he cannot catch all the children, that evil is ineradicable.

It is the final disillusionment, and dizzy with his terrible awareness, Holden insults Phoebe when she insists on running away with him. In his vision of despair, he sees Phoebe's irrevocable doom as well as his, and for a moment he hates her as he hates himself—as he hates the world. Once he has hurt her, however, he realizes the commitment that his love for her imposes on him; that is, if he is to palliate her pain, he must continue to live in the world. When she kisses him a few minutes later as a token of forgiveness and love, and as if in consequence it begins to rain, Holden, bathed by the rain, is purified—in a sense, redeemed. Like the narrator in "For Esmè

—With Love and Squalor," Holden is redeemed by the love of an innocent girl. In both cases the protagonist is saved because he realizes that if there is any love at all in the world, even the love of a single child, Love exists.

On its surface, the last scene, with Holden drenched in Scott Fitzgerald's all-absolving rain,[4] is unashamedly sentimental. Certainly Salinger overstates the curative powers of children; innocence can be destructive as well as redemptive. Yet for all that, Salinger's view of the universe, in which all adults, even the most apparently decent, are corrupt and consequently destructive, is bleak and somewhat terrifying. If growing up in the real world is tragic, in Salinger's ideal world time must be stopped to prevent the loss of childhood, to salvage the remnants of our innocence. At one point in the novel Holden wishes that life were as changeless and as pure as the exhibitions under glass cases in the Museum of Natural History. This explains, in part, Holden's ecstasy in the rain at the close of the novel. In watching Phoebe go round and round on the carousel, in effect going nowhere, he sees her in the timeless continuum of art, on the verge of changing, yet unchanging, forever safe, forever loving, forever innocent.

Salinger's view of the world has obviously limited his productiveness, also his range of concerns. In the last nine years he has published only four increasingly long, increasingly repetitive short stories, all treating some aspect of the mythic life and times of the Glass family, whose most talented member, Seymour, committed suicide in an early story called "A Perfect Day for Bananafish." But though Salinger may go on, as Hemingway did, mimicking himself, trying desperately to relocate his old youthful image in some narcissistic internal mirror, his achievement as a writer cannot be easily discounted. All his works, even the least successful of his stories, evince a stunning and, despite some stylistic debt to Fitzgerald and Lardner, original verbal talent. There is more real life in a small book like *The Catcher in the Rye* than in the combined pages of such a prolific and detailed chronicler of experience as John O'Hara.

4 It is the same symbolic rain that falls on Gatsby's coffin—at which Nick hears someone say, " 'Blessed are the dead whom the rain falls on.' " I suspect that Salinger had the Fitzgerald passage in mind.

Like *The Great Gatsby*, which both Holden and Salinger admire, it is, as far as the human eye can see, a perfect novel; it is self-defining; that is, there seems to be an inevitability about its form. Although the craft of the book is unobtrusive, everything of consequence that happens in the novel has been anticipated by an earlier episode or reference. Each of Holden's disillusioning experiences is predicated by the preceding one. The rain that baptizes Holden at the end is, in symbol, the same rain that had fallen on Allie's gravestone, which had depressed Holden because the visitors' scurry for shelter had served only to emphasize Allie's immobility, his deadness. In praying to Allie, Holden implicitly accepts the fact of his brother's immortality, which his earlier response had denied. Through association, Salinger suggests that the purifying rain is a manifestation of Allie's blessed and blessing spirit. Like Phoebe's kiss, Allie's rain is an act of love.

The near perfection of *The Catcher in the Rye* is indicative of its limitation as well as its achievement. Salinger knows what he can do well and he does it, taking a few indulgences of risk, but no more. On the other hand, men of comparable talent like William Styron and Norman Mailer have continually overreached themselves, have written both more ambitious and more flawed books than Salinger's only novel. It would be easy to quote from Browning's "Andrea del Sarto" and to insist that great literature, like great painting, must always attempt more than it can do, but the problem is not so easily resolvable. As a case in point: it would be hard to convince me that a small masterpiece like *The Great Gatsby* is less important than *Look Homeward Angel*, or even Fitzgerald's own larger failure, *Tender Is the Night*. Selective comparisons, of course, are hardly generative of final principles. In any event, it seems to me that Styron's extravagant failure *Set This House on Fire*, for example, is somewhat more admirable if not more important than Salinger's cautious success. Holden, I suspect, would understand what I mean.

5 · Nightmare of a Native Son:

Invisible Man by Ralph Ellison

> "Who knows but that, on the lower frequencies, I speak for you?"
>
> —*Invisible Man*

I HESITATE to call Ralph Ellison's *Invisible Man* (1953) a Negro novel, though of course it is written by a Negro and is centrally concerned with the experiences of a Negro. The appellation is not so much inaccurate as it is misleading. A novelist treating the invisibility and phantasmagoria of the Negro's life in this "democracy" is, if he tells the truth, necessarily writing a very special kind of book. Yet if his novel is interesting only because of its specialness, he has not violated the surface of his subject; he has not, after all, been serious. Despite the differences in their external concerns, Ellison has more in common as a novelist with Joyce, Melville, Camus, Kafka, West, and Faulkner than he does with other serious Negro writers like James Baldwin and Richard Wright. To concentrate on the idiom of a serious novel, no matter how distinctive its peculiarities, is to depreciate it, to minimize the universality of its implications. Though the protagonist of *Invisible Man* is a southern Negro, he is, in Ellison's rendering, profoundly all of us.

Despite its obvious social implications, Ellison's novel is a modern gothic, a Candide-like picaresque set in a dimly familiar nightmare landscape called the United States. Like *The Catcher in the Rye, A Member of the Wedding,* and *The Adventures of Augie March,* Ellison's novel chronicles a series of initiatory experiences through which its naïve hero learns, to his disillusion and horror, the way of the world. However, unlike these other novels of passage, *Invisible Man* takes place, for the most part, in the uncharted spaces between the conscious and the unconscious, in the semilit darkness where nightmare verges on reality and the external world has all the aspects of a disturbing dream. Refracted by satire, at times, cartooned, Ellison's world is at once surreal and real, comic and tragic, grotesque and normal— our world viewed in its essentials rather than its externals.

The Negro's life in our white land and time is, as Ellison knows it, a relentless unreality, unreal in that the Negro as a group is loved, hated, persecuted, feared, and envied, while as an individual he is unfelt, unheard, unseen—to all intents and purposes invisible. The narrator, who is also the novel's central participant, never identifies himself by name. Though he experiences several changes of identity in the course of the novel, Ellison's hero exists to the reader as a man without an identity, an invisible "I." In taking on a succession of identities, the invisible hero undergoes an increasingly intense succession of disillusioning experiences, each one paralleling and anticipating the one following it. The hero's final loss of illusion forces him underground into the coffin (and womb) of the earth to be either finally buried or finally reborn.

The narrator's grandfather, whom he resembles (identity is one of the major concerns of the novel), is the first to define the terms of existence for him. An apparently meek man all his life, on his deathbed the grandfather reveals:

> "Son, after I'm gone I want you to keep up the good fight. I never told you, but our life is a war and I have been a traitor all my born days, a spy in the enemy's country ever since I give up my gun back in the Reconstruction. Live with your head in the lion's mouth. I want you to overcome 'em with yesses, undermine 'em with grins, agree 'em to death and destruction, let 'em swoller you till they vomit or bust wide open." [1]

Though at the time he understands his grandfather's ambiguous creed only imperfectly, the hero recognizes that it is somehow his heritage. In a sense, the old man's code of acquiescent resistance is an involved justification of his nonresistance; it is a parody on itself, yet the possibility always remains that it is, in some profound, mysterious way, a meaningful ethic. On a succession of occasions, the hero applies his grandfather's ad-

[1] Ralph Ellison, *Invisible Man* (New York: New American Library, 1953), p. 19. All quotations are from this edition.

vice, "agreeing 'em to death," in order to understand its import through discovering its efficacy. On each occasion, however, it is he, not " 'em," who is victimized. Consequently, the hero suffers a sense of guilt—not for having compromised himself but for failing somehow to effect his grandfather's ends. Ironically, he also feels guilty for deceiving the white "enemy," though he has "agreed them" not to death or destruction, only to renewed complacency. For example:

When I was praised for my conduct I felt a guilt that in some way I was doing something that was really against the wishes of the white folks, that if they had understood they would have desired me to act just the opposite, that I should have been sulky and mean, and that really would have been what they wanted, even though they were fooled and thought they wanted me to act as I did. [p. 20]

The hero's cynical obsequiousness has self-destructive consequences. Having delivered a high school graduation speech advocating humility as the essence of progress, he is invited to deliver his agreeable oration to a meeting of the town's leading white citizens. Before he is allowed to speak, however, he is subjected to a series of brutal degradations, which teach him, in effect, the horror of the humility he advocates. In this episode, the first of his initiatory experiences, the invisible man's role is symbolically prophesied. The hero, along with nine other Negro boys, is put into a prize ring, then is blindfolded and coerced into battling his compatriots. Duped by the whites, the Negro unwittingly fights himself; his potency, which the white man envies and fears, is mocked and turned against him to satisfy the brutal whims of his persecutor. That the bout is is preceded by a nude, blond belly dancer whom the boys are forced to watch suggests the prurience underlying the victimizer's treatment of his victim. The degrading prizefight, a demonstration of potency to titillate the impotent, in which the Negro boys blindly flail one another to entertain the sexually aroused stag audience, parallels the riot in Harlem at the end of the novel, which is induced by another institution of white civilization, the Brotherhood (a fictional guise for the Communist party). Once again Negro fights against Negro (Ras the Destroyer against the hero), although this time it is for the sake of "Brotherhood," a euphemism for the same inhumanity. In both cases, the Negro unwittingly performs the obscene demands of his enemy. In magnification, Harlem is the prize ring where the Negroes, blindfolded this time by demagoguery, flail at each other with misdirected violence. The context has changed from South to North, from white citizens to the Brotherhood, from a hired ballroom to all of Harlem, but the implication remains the same: the Negro is victimized by having his potency turned against himself by his impotent persecutor.

After the boxing match, what appears to be gold is placed on a rug in the center of the room and the boys are told to scramble for their rewards. The hero reacts: "I trembled with excitement, forgetting my pain. I would get the gold and the bills, I thought. I would use both hands. I would throw my body against the boys nearest me to block them from the gold" (p. 29).

He is, on the rug as in the boxing ring, degraded by self-interest. Though his reaction is unpleasant, it is, given the provocation, the normal, calculable one. He has been tempted and, unaware of any practicable ethical alternative, has succumbed in innocence. When the temptation recurs in more complex guises later in the novel and Ellison's nameless hero as adult falls victim to his self-interest, he is, despite his larger moral purposes, culpable and must assume responsibility for the terrible consequences of his deeds. In each of the various analogous episodes, the hero is torn between his implicit commitment to his grandfather's position—subversive acquiescence —and his will to identity—the primal instinct of self-assertion. Both commitments dictate pragmatic, as opposed to purely ethical, action, with, inevitably, immoral and impractical consequences. The rug becomes electrified, the gold coins turn out to be brass—a means, like the bout, of mocking the Negro's envied potency. That the fight and electrification follow in sequence the naked belly dancer in the course of an evening of stag entertainment for tired white businessmen indicates the obscene prurience behind the white citizen's hatred of the Negro. By debasing and manipulating the Negro's potency, the white mutes its threat and at the same time experiences it

vicariously. It is in all a mordant evocation, satiric in its rendering and frightening in its implications. The white man's fascination with the Negro as a source of power (potency) is another
of the thematic threads that holds together what might otherwise be a picaresque succession of disparate episodes. The ballroom humiliation serves as a gloss on the following scene, in
which the hero is expelled from the Negro state college for,
ironically, the consequence of his obedience to a white trustee.

The president of the Negro college, Dr. Bledsoe (all of
Ellison's names characterize their bearers), entrusts the hero,
up to then a model student, with the responsibility of chauffeur-
ing a philanthropic white trustee, Mr. Norton, on a tour of the
manicured country surrounding the campus. Driving aimlessly
—or perhaps with more aim than he knows—the hero suddenly
discovers that he has taken the trustee to the backwoods home-
stead of Jim Trueblood, the area's black sheep, an "unen-
lightened" Negro whose sharecropper existence (and incestuous,
child producing, accident with his daughter) is a source of
continued embarrassment to the "progressive" community of
the college. The hero would like to leave, but Norton, curiously
fascinated by the fact that Trueblood has committed incest
(and survived), insists on talking with the sharecropper. At
Norton's prodding, Trueblood tells his story, an extended and
graphically detailed account of how he was induced by a dream
into having physical relations with his daughter. The story itself is a masterpiece of narrative invention and perhaps the
single most brilliant scene in the novel.

As Trueblood finishes his story, we discover in a moment of
ironic revelation that the bloodless Norton is a kind of euphemistic alter ego—a secret sharer—of the atavistic Trueblood.
Earlier, while being driven deeper into the backwoods country
—the reality behind the ivy league façade of the college—Norton
had rhapsodized to the narrator about the unearthly charms of
his own daughter, for whose death he feels unaccountably
guilty:

"Her beauty was a well-spring of purest water-of-life, and to look
upon her was to drink and drink and drink again. . . . She was
rare, a perfect creation, a work of purest art. . . . I found it difficult to believe her my own. . . ."

"I have never forgiven myself. Everything I've done since her passing has been a monument to her memory." [pp. 43–44]

Trueblood, then, has committed the very sin that Norton has, in the dark places of his spirit, impotently coveted. Upon hearing Trueblood's story, Norton participates vicariously in his experience, has his own quiescent desires fulfilled while exempted, since Trueblood has acted for him, from the stigma of the act. Underlying Norton's recurrent platitude that "the Negro is my fate" (he means that they are his potency) is the same prurience that motivates the sadism of the white citizens in the preceding scene. However, in an ironic way, Trueblood *is* Norton's fate. When Trueblood finishes his story, Norton feels compelled to pay him, as the white citizens reward the Negro boxers, in exchange for, in a double sense, having performed for him. When Norton (who exists here really as idea rather than character) leaves Trueblood's farm, he is exhausted and colorless, as if he had in fact just committed incest with his own daughter.

Having exposed Norton to the horror of his own philanthropic motives, after a further misadventure among inmates of a Negro insane asylum, the hero is expelled from school by Bledsoe because "any act that endangered the continuity of the dream is an act of treason." The boy, sensing his innocence, feels haunted by his grandfather's curse. Through Ellison's surrealistic rendering, we sense the nightmare reality of the hero's experience (as we do not with Norton's comparable nightmare):

How had I come to this? I had kept unswervingly to the path before me, had tried to be exactly what I was expected to be, had done exactly what I was expected to do—yet, instead of winning the expected reward, here I was stumbling along, holding on desperately to one of my eyes in order to keep from bursting out my brain against some familiar object swerved into my path by my distorted vision. And now to drive me wild I felt suddenly that my grandfather was hovering over me, grinning triumphantly out of the dark. [p. 131]

Accepting responsibility for the sins of his innocence, the hero goes to New York, armed with several letters of "identification" which Bledsoe has addressed to various trustees for the ostensible purpose of finding him a job. When the hero discovers that the letters have been written "to hope him to death, and keep him running," that the renowned Negro educator Bledsoe has betrayed him treacherously, has in effect ordered him killed as an almost gratuitous display of power, he experiences a moment of terrible disillusion. At the same time he senses that this betrayal is in some way a re-enactment of the past: "Twenty-five years seemed to have lapsed between his handing me the letter and my grasping its message. I could not believe it, yet I had a feeling that it all had happened before. I rubbed my eyes, and they felt sandy as though all the fluids had suddenly dried" (p. 168).

In a way, it *has* happened before; for Bledsoe's act of victimization (the beating of Negro by Negro) is analogous to the punishment the hero received in the prize ring at the hands of the largest of the other Negro boys. Bledsoe's deceit, like its analog, is motivated by the desire to ingratiate himself with the white society which dispenses rewards—which provides, or so he believes, the source of his power.

As one episode parallels another, each vignette in itself has allegorical extensions. Employed by Liberty Paints, a factory "the size of a small city," the narrator is ordered to put ten drops of "black dope" into buckets of optic white paint in order, he is told, to make it whiter. The mixing of the black into the white is, of course, symbolic: the ten drops are analogous to the ten boys in the prize ring, and in each case the white becomes whiter by absorbing the Negro's virility, by using the black to increase the strength of the white. Yet the name "optic white" suggests it is all some kind of visual illusion. When the black dope runs out, the hero as apprentice paint mixer is ordered by his boss, "the terrible Mr. Kimbro," to replace it, without being told which of seven possible vats has the right substance. Left to his own discretion, the hero chooses the wrong black liquid, concentrated paint remover, which makes the white paint transparent and grayish; this act symbolizes the implicit threat of Negro potency left to its own devices. The paint-mixing scene is paralleled by the violence of the insane Negro veterans at the bar (the Golden Day) in which they beat their white attendant Supercargo into grayness and terrorize the already depleted Norton. It anticipates the antiwhite violence of Ras the exhorter-turned-destroyer, the only alternative to invisibility the white man has left the Negro.

Yet there is the illusion of another alternative: when the narrator adds the black drops to the paint which already contains the black remover, though the mixture appears gray to him, it passes for white in Kimbro's eyes. This is, in symbol, the role of subterfuge and infiltration—his grandfather's legacy and curse.

> I looked at the painted slab. It appeared the same: a gray tinge glowed through the whiteness, and Kimbro had failed to detect it. I stared for a minute, wondering if I were seeing things, inspected another and another. All were the same, a brilliant white diffused with gray. I closed my eyes for a moment and looked again and still no change. Well, I thought as long as he's satisfied. . . . [p. 180]

Kimbro permits the gray-tinged paint to be shipped out and the hero wonders whether, after all, he has been the deceiver or the deceived. He suspects, when Kimbro dismisses him, that he somehow has been the dupe. That the paint passes for white in Kimbro's eyes suggests that the black with which it was mixed was, like the hero's existence, to all intents and purposes, invisible.

Essentially invisible, the narrator undergoes a succession of superficial changes of identity—in a sense, changes of mask—each entailing a symbolic, though illusory, death and rebirth. Knocked unconscious by the explosion of a machine which makes the base of a white paint, a machine that he was unable to control, the hero is placed in another machine, a coffin-like electrified box, in order to be "started again." The shock treatments surrealistically rendered recall the electrification from the rug, however magnified in intensity. Like most of the episodes in the novel, it is on the surface a comic scene, though in its implications (lobotomy and castration) it is a singularly unpleasant nightmare. The hero's first awareness upon awakening is that he is enclosed in a glass box with an electric cap attached to his head, a combination coffin-womb and electrocutor. When he is blasted with a charge of electricity, he instinctively screams in agonized protest, only to be told in response as if he were indeed a piece of equipment, " 'Hush goddamit . . . We're trying to get you started again. Now shut up!' " (p. 203). After a while he is unable to remember who he is or whether he has in fact existed before his present moment of consciousness: "My mind was blank, as though I'd just begun to live." Like the charged rug, though considerably more cruel, the shock treatments are intended to neutralize him, in effect to castrate him. In his moments of confused consciousness he hears two voices arguing over the proper method to treat his case. One is in favor of surgery, the other in favor of the machine.

"The machine will produce the results of a prefrontal lobotomy without the negative effect of the knife," the voice said. "You see, instead of severing the prefrontal lobe, a single lobe, that is, we apply pressure in the proper degrees to the major centers of nerve control—our concept is Gestalt—and the result is as complete a change of personality as you'll find in your famous fairy-tale cases of criminals transformed into amiable fellows after all that bloody business of a brain operation. And what's more," the voice went on triumphantly, "the patient is both physically and neurally whole."

"But what of his psychology?"

"Absolutely of no importance!" the voice said. "The patient will live as he has to live, with absolute integrity. Who could ask more? He'll experience no major conflict of motives, and what is even better, society will suffer no traumata on his account."

There was a pause. A pen scratched upon paper. Then, "Why not castration, doctor?" a voice asked waggishly, causing me to start, a pain tearing through me.

"There goes your love of blood again," the first voice laughed. "What's that definition of a surgeon, 'A butcher with a bad conscience'?"

They laughed. [pp. 206–207]

I quote this passage at length to suggest the high-voltage charge of Ellison's satire, capable at once of being mordantly comic and profoundly terrifying. The clinical attitude of the psychologist ("society will suffer no traumata on his account") suggests the northern white position toward the Negro, as opposed to the butcher-surgeon who represents the more overtly violent southern position. The ends of both, however, are approxi-

mately the same—emasculation; the difference is essentially one
of means.

The narrator is, in this scene, almost visibly invisible, discussed impersonally in his presence as if he were not there.
When he is unable to recall his name, his mother's name, any
form of his identity, any form of his past, the doctors seem
pleased and deliver him from the machine, the only mother he
knows.

> I felt a tug at my belly and looked down to see one of the
> physicians pull the cord which was attached to the stomach node,
> jerking me forward. . . .
> "Get the shears," he said. "Let's not waste time."
> "Sure," the other said. "Let's not waste time."
> I recoiled inwardly as though the cord were part of me. Then
> they had it free and the nurse clipped through the belly band and
> removed the heavy node. [p. 213]

In describing the birth from the machine, Ellison suggests
through evocation that it is also a kind of castration. Insofar as
it leaves the hero without the potency of self, it is, in implication, just that.

Aside from the Prologue and parts of the Epilogue, which
have an enlightened madness all their own, the experience of
the machine birth is the least realistic, the most surrealistic, in
the novel. And this brings us to what I think is the novel's
crucial flaw, its inconsistency of method, its often violent trans-
formations from a kind of detailed surface realism in which
probability is limited to the context of ordinary, everyday experiences to an allegorical world of almost endless imaginative
possibilities. Often the shift is dramatically effective, as when
the hero and Norton enter the insane world of the Golden Day
(here the truth is illuminated by a nominal madman who has
the insane virtue of pure sight) and Norton is forced into a
frightening moment of self-recognition. On other occasions, the
visional shifts jar us away from the novel's amazing world into
an awareness of the ingenuity of its creator. Since Ellison is at
once prodigiously talented and prodigiously reckless, *Invisible
Man* is astonishingly good at its best. By the same token the
book is uneven; on occasion it is very bad as only very good

novels can be. Given the nature of his vision, Ellison's world seems real—or alive—when it is surrealistically distorted, and for the most part made-up—or abstract—when it imitates the real world. Largely recounted in the manner of traditional realism, the hero's adventures in the Brotherhood up until the Harlem riot constitute the least interesting section of the novel.

In joining the Brotherhood, the narrator gives up his past to assume a new identity or rather new nonidentity, Brother ————. Because of his remarkable speech-making abilities, as well as his conscious ambition to be some kind of savior, he becomes one of the leading figures of the Harlem Brotherhood. Finally, his controversial activities make it necessary for him to disguise himself in order to get through Harlem safely. Brother ————'s disguise—dark glasses and a wide-brimmed hat—which he has hoped would make him inconspicuous in Harlem, creates for him still another identity, which is, in effect, just a new aspect of nonidentity. Wearing the hat and glasses, Brother ———— is unrecognized as his Brotherhood self, but is mistaken for a man named Rinehart, a charlatan of incredible diversification. Rinehart, whose identities include numbers runner, police briber, lover, pimp, and Reverend, is, the hero discovers, a kind of alter ego to his invisibility. If you are no one, you are at the same time potentially everyone. The hero has disguised himself in order to avoid the consequences of his acts and instead finds himself held responsible for Rinehart's inordinate sins—for all sins—which are, in the Dostoyevskian sense, his own. When the Brotherhood's theoretician Hambro informs the hero that, with the alteration of the larger plan, his role has changed from exhorter to pacifier, he senses his likeness to his dazzling alter ego:

". . . Besides I'd feel like Rinehart. . . ." It slipped out and he looked at me.
"Like who?"
"Like a charlatan," I said.
Hambro laughed. "I thought you learned about that, Brother."
I looked at him quickly. "Learned what?"
"That it's impossible *not* to take advantage of the people."
"That's Rinehartism—cynicism. . . ." [p. 436]

In following the dictates of the Brotherhood, the hero has hurt, he discovers to his pain, the very people he has intended to help. Without benefit of glasses and hat, he has been a Rinehart in disguise all the time. He has been, paradoxically, an unwitting cynic. Duped by his self-conscious, romantic ambitions to be another Booker T. Washington, the hero has let the Brotherhood use him for their cynical "historic" purposes. As a Brotherhood agent, he demagogically incites the Harlem Negroes to potential action only to leave them prey to the misdirected violence of Ras, their violence ultimately turned, like that of the boys in the prize ring, against themselves. With awareness comes responsibility, and the hero recognizes that he alone must bear the guilt for the Brotherhood's betrayal of the Negro. The ramifications of his awful responsibility are manifested generally in the hellish Harlem riot at the end of the novel and particularly in the disillusion and death of the most admirable of the Brotherhood, Tod Clifton (the name suggests a kind of Promethean entrapment), whose career prophesies and parallels that of the hero.

Earlier in the novel, Ras, after sparing Tod's life, has exhorted his adversary to leave the Brotherhood and join his racist movement (a fictionalized version of the Black Muslims). Their confrontation, an objectification of the hero's interior struggle, anticipates Tod's defection from the Brotherhood.

"Come with us, mahn. We build a glorious movement of black people. *Black people!* What do they do, give you money? Who wahnt the damn stuff? Their money bleed black blood, mahn. It's unclean! Taking their money is shit, mahn. Money without dignity—that's *bahd* shit!"

Clifton lunged toward him. I held him, shaking my head. "Come on, the man's crazy," I said, pulling on his arm.

Ras struck his thighs with his fists. "Me crazy, mahn? You call me crazy? Look at you two and look at me—is this sanity? Standing here in three shades of blackness! Three black men fighting in the street because of the white enslaver? Is that sanity? Is that consciousness, scientific understanding? Is that the modern black mahn of the twentieth century? Hell, mahn! Is it self-respect—black against black? What they give you to betray—their women? You fall for that?"

"Let's go," I repeated. He stood there, looking.

"Sure, you go," Ras said, "but not him. You contahminated but he the real black mahn. In Africa this mahn be a chief, a black king!" [pp. 322–23]

In this eloquent scene, Clifton finally rejects Ras, but he is undeniably moved by his enemy's crude exhortation. Ras—the name suggests an amalgam of race and rash—is a fanatic, but given his basic premise, that the white man is the Negro's natural enemy, his arguments are not easily refutable. Unable to answer Ras, Clifton, out of a sense of shame or guilt, knocks the Exhorter down, committing an act of Rasian violence. The punch is an acknowledgment, a communion, an act of love. As they leave, the hero discovers that Clifton has tears in his eyes. Clifton says, referring to Ras, " 'That poor misguided son of a bitch.' 'He thinks a lot of you, too,' I said" (p. 326).

Clifton is sympathetic to Ras's motives, but he is nevertheless too civilized to accept his methods. The Brotherhood, then, with its cant of "historic necessity," represents to Clifton the enlightened alternative to racist violence through which the Negro can effect his protest. Entrapped by the Brotherhood through the commitment imposed by his integrity, Clifton becomes, even more than the narrator, a victim of the Brotherhood's betrayal. Like the implicit suicide of Conrad's Lord Jim, Clifton's death (he provokes a policeman into shooting him) is a sacrifice to a culpability too egregious to be redeemed in any other way, and, at the same time, a final if gratuitous act of heroism. In giving himself up to be murdered, Clifton takes on the whole responsibility for the Brotherhood's betrayal of the Negro. If by his sacrifice he does not redeem the hero from his own culpability, he at least through his example sets up the possibility of Brother ———'s redemption. If the various characters with whom the "invisible" hero is confronted represent possible states of being, Clifton symbolizes the nearest thing to an ideal.

Clifton's death, because it permits the hero to organize the Negroes around a common cause (the narrator's funeral oration is a magnificent parody of Antony's), is potentially an agency of good, for Clifton can be considered in a meaningful sense a sacrifice. However, even that is denied him. At the last minute the Brotherhood withdraws its support from the hero, and, left to their own devices and the exhortation of Ras, the aroused Negroes perform arbitrary acts of plunder and violence. That Clifton's death initiates the Harlem riots, which serve the Brotherhood's new purpose of pacifying the Negro by exhausting his hate-charged energies in meaningless self-conflict, is a last terrible mockery of his decent intentions.

In hawking the chauvinistic "Sambo dolls" which dance at the tug of an invisible string, Clifton was not so much mocking the Brotherhood's attitude toward the Negro as he was parodying himself. His own comment about Ras suggests in a way the impulse of his nihilistic act:

> "I don't know," he said. "I suppose sometimes a man *has* to plunge outside history. . . ."
> "What?"
> "Plunge outside, turn his back. . . . Otherwise, he might kill somebody, go nuts." [p. 328]

Deceived by the bogus historians of the Brotherhood, Clifton has "plunged outside history," though in punching the white policeman he demonstrated that he had not quite "turned his back." As an alternative to violent reprisal—Clifton was an essentially gentle man racked by rage—he became a heckler of the Brotherhood, of the Negro, of the white man's treatment of the Negro, of himself, of the universe. Though he is one of the few noble characters in Ellison's world, his destruction is less than tragic. A man of tragic stature, Clifton is a captive participant in an absurd world which derogates him and mocks the significance of his death as it did his life. Clifton's sacrificial act, its intention perverted, is mostly invisible. The others of the Brotherhood—Wrestrum (rest room), Tobitt (two bit), Jack (money, masturbation)—who in their commitment to "science" have become as dehumanized and corrupt as those they oppose, survive the shift in tactical policy.

When the hero discovers that it is through him that the Brotherhood has betrayed Clifton, he feels responsible for his friend's death. Earlier, in outrage he spat at one of Clifton's dancing puppets, knocking it "lifeless," performing symbolically what the policeman does actually—the murder of Clifton. When the hero knocks over the doll, an onlooker laughs at what he thinks is the likeness between the spitter and the spat-on doll. Just as Clifton in selling the obscene doll has been mocking himself, the hero in spitting at the doll has been attacking himself as well as Clifton, though without benefit of awareness. Only after his showdown with the Brotherhood, and even then incompletely, does the hero become aware that he has been performing all along as if he were, in life size, the dancing puppet doll.

At his moment of greatest self-awareness, the hero suffers his most intense sense of guilt. Watching two nuns in the subway (one black, one white), he remembers a ritual verse he had once heard.

> Bread and wine,
> Bread and wine,
>   Your cross ain't nearly so
>   Heavy as mine. . . . [p. 382]

The rhyme comes to him as an automatic response, its singsong at first over-riding its sense. Momentarily, almost without wareness, as the pain of wound travels from flesh to brain, he comes to assume its implications. As he watches some Negroes maltreat a white shopkeeper, he experiences a terrible revelation:

A pressure of guilt came over me. I stood on the edge of the walk watching the crowd threatening to attack the man until a policeman appeared and dispersed them. And although I knew no one could do much about it, I felt responsible. All our work had been very little, no great change had been made. And it was all my fault. I'd been so fascinated by the motion that I'd forgotten to measure what it was bringing forth. I'd been asleep, dreaming. [p. 384]

A sleepwalker in a world never real enough for him to believe in, the hero experiences a succession of awakenings, only to find himself participating in still another level of nightmare. In accepting Clifton's role as martyr-saint, in taking on the responsibility for all of Harlem, all of Brotherhood, in extension, *all*, he succeeds only in setting himself up for a final, self-destroying victimization. Aware of the futility of all his past acts and, in implication, all acts in the absurd context of his world, the hero commits an act of meaningless violence. Entrapped by a situation for which he is at least partly responsible, with his neck quite literally at stake (Ras wants to hang him), he impales the demonic innocent, Ras, through the jaw with his own spear.

That Jack, the leader of the Brotherhood, has one eye (as earlier the eumphemistic preacher Barbee is revealed as blind) is symbolic of the distorted perspective of the Brotherhood's "scientifically objective view" of society, in which the human being is a casual puppet in the service of the "historic" strings that manipulate him. Clifton makes only *paper* Negroes dance; it is Jack and Tobitt who treat flesh-and-blood Negroes as if they were puppet Sambo dolls. (By having Clifton charge a "brotherly two bits" for the puppet dolls, Ellison, through suggestion, transfers the onus of traitor to Tobitt and in extension to the Brotherhood itself.) When the hero discovers that the Brotherhood has betrayed him, he consciously resolves to impersonate the puppet doll he has so long mimicked unwittingly —to, as his grandfather advised, "overcome 'em with yeses . . . agree 'em to death and destruction." For all his Rinehartian machinations, he manages, however, only to abet the scheme of the Brotherhood.

Seeking redemption from his compounded guilt, he is sucked into the malestrom of the Harlem riot for which he suffers a sense of limitless, unreclaimable responsibility. He realizes that "By pretending to agree I had indeed agreed, had made myself responsible for that huddled form lighted by flame and gunfire in the street, and all others whom now the night was making ripe for death" (p. 478). The flaming buildings and streets, the burnt tar stench, the black figures moving shadowlike through the eerily illumined night become an evocation of Hell, a mirror for the hero's raging interior guilt. At the center of the riot—at the very seat of Hell—he experiences the deaths of his various corrupted identities, shedding the false skins to get at the pure invisibility underneath. As Ras approaches, the hero searches for his "Rineharts," his dark glasses, only to "see the crushed lenses fall to the street. " 'Rinehart, I thought, Rinehart!' " as if he had just witnessed Rinehart himself—his Rinehart self—collapse in death before him. To propitiate Ras and stop the riots, the hero disavows allegiance to the Brotherhood, killing in effect his Brotherhood self. But as he is invisible, he is unheard, his words as always not communicating his meanings. Struck by the ab-

surdity of the demonic Ras on horseback, of the senseless pil-
lage and murder around him, and, after all, of existence itself,
the hero is for the moment willing to relinquish his life if it will
make the white man see him and consequently see himself. But
the example of Clifton's meaningless sacrifice dissuades him.
The hero, faced with death, decides that it is "better to live out
one's own absurdity than to die for that of others, whether for
Ras's or Jack's." When in self-protection he impales Ras, who
is in a sense the deepest of his identities, he experiences the
illusion of death and rebirth: "It was as though for a
moment I had surrendered my life and begun to live again"
(p. 484).

Newly baptized by an exploded water main, like the birth
from the machine, a somewhat illusory (and comic) resurrection, the hero seeks to return to Mary, his exlandlady, who has
become a symbolic mother to him. But as he is unable to imi-
tate Christ, he is unable to reach Mary. Instead, chased by two
white looters, he falls though an open manhole. Unable to find
the exit to his coffinlike cell, he burns various papers of his
past (high school diploma, Sambo doll, Brotherhood card) for
torches to light his way out, only to discover in a moment of
terrible realization that the Jacks and Nortons have left him
no exit, that without his paper symbols he has no past and
consequently no home, no identity. With this knowledge he
relaxes in the carrion comfort of his dank hole, having returned
at last to the womb of the earth. It is, as he puts it, a "death
alive," from which emergence will be rebirth, his victimization
transcended, his guilt perhaps purged, his soul if possible redeemed. A nonparticipant in existence, an invisible man by
choice, the hero continues to live in his private cellar, which
he has illumined by 1,369 lights (a symbolic attempt at tran-
scending his invisibility—at seeing himself), the electricity sup-
plied gratuitously in spite of themselves by Monopolated Light
and Power. As the whites had mocked his potency and used it
for their own ends, he is now paying them back in kind. Though
he is protected from the pain of disillusion while isolated from
the brutal, absurd world he hates and, in spite of himself, loves,
the hero plans some day to emerge into the outside world because, a son of God and man, one of us, he is willing to believe

that "even the invisible victim is responsible for the fate of all" (p. 487).

Much of the experience in Ellison's novel is externally imposed; that is, each scene, through allusive reference, is made to carry a burden of implication beyond that generated by its particular experience. Consequently the weight of the novel, its profound moral seriousness, resides primarily in conception rather than rendering. Given the problem of transforming large abstractions into evocative experiences, Ellison is nevertheless able more often than not to create occasions resonant enough to accommodate his allegorical purposes. Finally, one senses that the novel, for all its picaresque variety of incident, has a curiously static quality. This is not because the episodes are the same or even similar—on the contrary, one is compelled to admire the range and resourcefulness of Ellison's imaginative constructions—but because they are all extensions of the same externally imposed idea; they all *mean* approximately the same thing.

Like so many of our serious writers, Ellison is not prolific. It took him, by his own testimony, some seven years to write *Invisible Man*, and now eleven years after its publication his second novel is still not completed. If Ellison's reputation had to rest, as it does at the time of this writing, on his one impressive if uneven novel, *Invisible Man* is, I suspect, vital and profound enough to survive its faults—to endure the erosions of time. As a satirist and surrealist, Ellison excels among his contemporaries and can bear comparison with his mentors—Kafka, Joyce, and Faulkner. As a realist, he is less adept: talky, didactic, even at times, if the term is possible for so otherwise exciting a writer, tedious. For all that, Ellison has written a major novel, perhaps one of the three or four most considerable American novels of the past two decades.

An excerpt from his forthcoming novel, "And Hickman Arrives," published in the first issue of *The Noble Savage*, exhibits some of the same evangelical rhetoric that gives *Invisible Man* its terrible impact. Still, it is idle from a fifty-page fragment to prophesy what kind of novel it will make. Moreover, "And Hickman Arrives" has many of the damaging excesses of the first novel. Ellison has a penchant for letting good things go on past their maximum effectiveness. Yet his excesses are also his strength; like Faulkner before him, Ellison is a writer of amazing verbal energy and at his best he creates experiences that touch our deepest selves, that haunt us with the suffocating wisdom of nightmare. American novelists have often had a predilection for large, protracted books, as if great length were a virtue in itself. Ellison is no exception. However, he is one of the few novelists on the scene today who seems capable of producing a large, serious novel, justified by the size of its experience and the depth of its informing intelligence. On the lowest (and highest) frequencies, he speaks for us.

6 · The Acid of God's Grace:

Wise Blood by Flannery O'Connor

> God's grace burns.
> —*The Violent Bear it Away.*

> Redemption is meaningless unless there is
> cause for it in the actual life we live, and for
> the last few centuries there has been operat-
> ing in our culture the secular belief that there
> is no such cause.
> —Flannery O'Connor in *The Living Novel*

THAT Flannery O'Connor was a strikingly original talent hardly
needs saying. Yet because of the specialness of her fictional
world—the gothic scenery, the grotesque comedy, the gratuitous
violence, the religiosity—she has been overpraised and over-
damned without, it seems to me, being properly understood.
With rare exception, Miss O'Conner explored in all her fiction
the same private world, a world of corrosion and decay, invested
with evil, apparently God-forsaken, but finally redeemed by
God. Despite her somewhat solemn concerns, at her best her
fiction is mordantly comic. The practice of life is an eternally
serious business, but the world which gives it occasion is a
grotesque and absurd place.

Since all of Flannery O'Connor's work, *Wise Blood* (1952),
The Violent Bear It Away (1961), and the short story collection, *A Good Man Is Hard to Find* (1956), has the same rigidly
defined religious concerns, the same theological pattern, I will
limit myself to a close reading of her remarkable first novel
Wise Blood in an attempt to define in concentration the quality
and impulse of her fictional art. A highly specialized initiatory
ritual takes place in both of Miss O'Connor's novels which are
more explicitly religious than most of the stories. The ritual
configuration is a reversal of the *rite de passage*; that is, her central characters do not fall from innocence. They are fallen from
the outset and move, doomed, through an infested world pro-
liferating its evils, until at the heart of darkness they discover
light, or God, and through renunciation and extreme penance

achieve redemption for themselves and, in extension, for all of us. Hazel Motes in *Wise Blood*, like Tarwater in *The Violent Bear It Away*, is by metaphysical ordination a man of God (each protagonist is the grandson of a preacher) who resists His calling only to discover God at last in an awesome revelation.

During his term in the army, Haze, disillusioned by the existence of evil in the world, sins for the first time. As a consequence he denies Christ in order to justify his behavior and then continues to sin in order to justify his unbelief. To whoever will listen, and to some who won't, Haze preaches against redemption, insistently and obsessively denying Jesus. At the start of the novel, approaching a woman on a train: " 'Do you think I believe in Jesus?' he said leaning toward her and speaking almost as if he were breathless. 'Well I wouldn't even if He existed. Even if he were on this train.' " [1]

The frantic insistence with which Haze preaches against Jesus suggests the depth of his religiosity, his inescapable involvement with the Christ image. Haze blasphemes, seeking proof and reproof, seeking his own salvation. The novel's irony resides in that no one is willing to save him, that his blasphemy passes virtually unnoticed. In Miss O'Connor's world, a sea of evil, one more iniquitous drop is hardly perceptible. No one will redeem Haze, he must redeem himself; he must transform his life in Christ's image, which means a self-crucifixion. It is the only redemptive possibility in a depraved world. At the end, Haze immolates himself, re-enacting, in effect, the redemption of Man.

If God does not exist, Haze decides at the outset of the novel (as Ivan Karamazov had before him), there can be no sin—everything is permissible. In order to demonstrate his position, Haze determinedly sins even—and this is the irony of his behavior—when his nature revolts against the act: "He felt that he should have a woman, not for the sake of the pleasure in her, but to prove that he didn't believe in sin since he practiced what was called it" (p. 110). The commission of sin becomes for Haze a kind of ritual declaration of freedom from

---

[1] Flannery O'Connor, *Wise Blood* (New York: Harcourt, Brace & World, Inc., 1952), p. 16. All quotations are from this edition.

God the Father's authority. Ironically, the more Haze sins, the
more committed he becomes to the import of His judgment.
His first conscious act in Taulkinham (the big city) is to visit
a prostitute recommended to him by a brotherly notice on the
wall of a toilet booth:

> Mrs. Leora Watts
> 60 Buckley Road
> The friendliest bed in town!
> Brother [p. 30]

In a city in which human communication is limited to expediency, deception, murder, and violation, the prostitute's bed
is the friendliest in town; it is in any event the most honest. For
all of Haze's insistence that he believes in nothing, he is unable
to act without recriminations of guilt. His sinning is an insistent
denial of the God in him and is self-mortifying, pleasurable
only in a masochistic sense. No matter what he does to change
his appearance, his calling evinces itself; he is unmistakably a
preacher. Haunted by unadmitted guilt, Haze is constrained
to deny his identity. His denial, because of its very insistence,
becomes an affirmation. He informs Mrs. Watts, though she
hasn't asked him, " 'What I mean to have you know is: I'm no
goddam preacher.' Mrs. Watts eyed him steadily with only a
slight smirk. Then she put her other hand under his face and
tickled it in a motherly way. 'That's okay, son,' she said.
'Momma don't mind if you ain't a preacher' " (p. 34). Haze
can't escape himself or his destiny. As he performs it, even
whoring becomes a religious act, a kind of penitential sin. He
sins, hoping in his punishment to discover the vengeance and
mercy of God.

In his search for salvation, Haze is continually confronted
by the disparity between appearance and reality. God in
Taulkinham is nowhere manifested. Haze is repeatedly con-
firmed in his anti-Christian course of action, though he knows
instinctively that he is wrong. When he meets a blind preacher
with his little girl, Haze follows them, bent on his own salvation. That the preacher's name is Hawks and that he is intro-
duced competing for disciples with a salesman hawking potato
peelers suggests the essential likeness between the two—the

shared corruption. The blind preacher and the girl are not what they seem: the man is neither blind nor a man of God; the girl is not a child but an ugly and parasitic slut. They are both, as Hawks, predatory, selling salvation as if man were as easily shriven as a potato is peeled. While Asa Hawks preaches of Christ without believing in Him, Haze, who profoundly believes, preaches of "the church of truth without Jesus Christ Crucified." However, in a causal sense, the spurious blind man is Haze's spiritual father. The lustful girl, Sabbath Hawks, one of the prize grotesques in Miss O'Connor's gallery of moral deformities, woos Haze by taking advantage of his attraction to her "father's" ostensible religiosity. She gets Hawks to show Haze the first of his two newspaper clippings—"EVANGELIST PROMISES TO BLIND HIMSELF"—which describes how Hawks had volunteered to burn out his eyes publicly as proof of his redemption. The second clipping, which is withheld from Haze, describes how Hawks had lost his nerve and scarred his face with the lime but spared his eyes. The act, though unenacted, deeply, indelibly impresses Hazel, becomes his legacy. At the last, unable to bear the sight of evil any longer, he fulfills Hawks' forsaken intention—he burns out his own eyes.

There are two central characters in Wise Blood, Hazel Motes and Enoch Emery, whose careers are parallel, the life of one prefiguring that of the other. Enoch, whom Hazel meets in front of the street hawker, is his comic counterpart. Throughout the novel Miss O'Connor suggests, through the use of various double images (Dostoevskian alter egos), the profound possibilities of good and evil in each man, that man is a kind of internal Manichean. While Haze seeks Jesus, or proof of His existence, Enoch seeks a friend, any friend, and Haze seems to him as apt a prospect as any. Hanging on to Haze's sleeve, Enoch pleads for companionship, for recognition. As he tells Haze, " 'I ain't but eighteen year old . . . and I don't know nobody, nobody here'll have nothing to do with nobody else. They ain't friendly.' " Haze is too self-obsessed to be moved by the repulsive Enoch's pleas, but Enoch persists, assured in his "wise blood" that there is some mystic connection between them. When Haze and Hawks confront each other for the first time in a debate over the existence of Jesus, Enoch, insisting on his own existence, intrudes irrelevantly:

> "I know a whole heap about Jesus," Enoch said. "I attended thisyer Rodemill Boys' Bible Academy that a woman sent me to. If it's anything you want to know about Jesus, just ast me." [p. 51]

Enoch's knowledge of Jesus is an extension into absurdity of the empty, euphemistic posture of organized religion, symbolized by the "Jesus Saves" signs overlooking the desolation and corrupton of the Georgia roads. Professional religiosity in Miss O'Connor's world manifests itself in grotesque hypocrisies, often malevolently cynical and profane. Enoch's career, his "change of life," not only prefigures Haze's but parodies it. In consequence, it parodies the empty ritual of contemporary God-hawking, redemption qua redemption, painless salvation for the masses—regardless of race, creed, or spirituality. Enoch's spiritual rebirth through the "new Jesus" (a shrunken mummy), his transformation from man into gorilla, is a satiric inversion of the evolutionary process.[2] His redemption is a grotesque joke, the ultimate absurdity of meretricious religiosity, but like everything else in the novel it is meant in dead earnest. As Milton's Satan, in transforming himself into a snake, unwittingly manifests the physical equivalent of his corrupted spirit, so Enoch, in assuming the gorilla suit, discovers his true identity. Like Hazel's mortification at the end of the novel, Enoch's is an exemplary act, an objectified comment on the spiritual state of his society. He is our clown, our patsy, our butt; but the joke is, of course, on all of us.

Enoch is a comic figure; Haze, a tragic. They are each in a special sense redeemers: Enoch, a mock redeemer; Haze, a real one. The interconnection of their destinies is the unifying concern of the novel. As it is, the two parallel "lives" often seem only parallel, as if the world of one were an intrusion on the world of the other. Conversations between Enoch and Hazel have the quality of a split-screen television discussion where the two participants are actually 3,000 miles apart. When Enoch hears his alter ego Haze preaching in front of a movie theater:

2 Miss O'Connor's joke on the evolutionary process has its analog in Huxley's *After Many a Summer Dies the Swan.*

"The Church Without Christ don't have a Jesus but it needs one! It needs one that's all man, without blood to waste, and it needs one that don't look like any other man so you'll look at him. Give me such a jesus you people. Give me such a new jesus and you'll see how far the Church Without Christ can go!" [pp. 140–41]

his "wise blood" tingles with revelation; Enoch knows where to find the "new jesus" Hazel's church requires. At the zoo where Enoch works there is a museum which contains, among other glass-encased curiosities, a "dried yellow" mummy shrunken by some Arabs, the caption reports, from normal height to his present three-foot length satisfying all the particulars of Hazel's description of his new savior. For some time, Enoch has kept secret his religious intuition about the mummy, waiting for the right occasion to reveal it. His "friend" Hazel provides the occasion and Enoch steals the "new jesus" for him so that he may set it up in his "Church Without Christ" (With New Christ). The shrunken creature is for Enoch an objectification of his deformed spirit, and in offering it to Hazel he is in effect offering himself. Hazel rejects the gift as he has rejected Enoch.

Unable to reach his preacher friend, Enoch delivers the mummy to Sabbath Hawks, who has moved in with Hazel. Before Hazel discovers the "new jesus," the evil girl has learned to dote on it, playing house with it as if it were child of her union with Hazel. In more than one sense, however, the creature does ultimately save Hazel; it gives him his first recognition of objectified evil, and he sees it as the manifest offspring of his sins, mocking him. He also recognizes it as himself—his double. Wearing his mother's glasses, he sees his own image in the mirror as his mother's, when images of Sabbath and the mummy merge into his mirror vision, blurring all distinctions. He hears a voice saying, "Call me Momma now," and is confronted by the screwed-up face of the shrunken creature. His smashing of the mummy against the wall is his first self-murder; it prophesies and anticipates Hazel's brutal murder of his double, the false preacher, whom Hoover Shoats has hired to impersonate Hazel. In killing his impersonator (Haze's evil self), Haze, in a sense, purges his evil, making possible his rebirth and final redemption. Whereas Enoch, through the "new jesus" and through the murder of his alter ego, is reborn into seeming innocence—his redemption a joke on itself, Haze is reborn through his ultimate evil act into self-knowledge and, ironically, innocence, becoming in effect the "new jesus" himself, sacrificing himself for his belief in the redemption of Christ.

Much the funniest scene in the novel is Enoch's first confrontation with Gonga, the gorilla movie star. Enoch, lonely and unloved, envies the zoo animals the comfort and attention they receive. Of the possibilities imaginable to him, the carefree caged existence of the zoo inhabitants seems to him ideal, and he passionately resents the fact that they (the less deserving) are on the inside while he is on the out. He sees his opportunity for revenge when he learns that Gonga, the most successful of all gorillas, will appear in person at local movie houses to shake hands with all his friends and admirers. Enoch waits in line behind a bevy of small children, searching his soul for the properly devastating insult with which to deflate his natural enemy. However, when the gorilla finally grips his hand, Enoch is disarmed by the creature's warmth and friendship; the gorilla's is the first friendly hand Enoch has grasped since coming to the big city:

For a second he only stood there, clasping it. Then he began to stammer. "My name is Enoch Emery," he mumbled. "I attended the Rodemill Boy's Bible Academy. I work at the city zoo. I seen two of your pictures. I'm only eighteen year old but I already work for the city. My daddy made me com . . ." and his voice cracked. [p. 182]

Enoch's confession leaks out like the gasoline from Haze's holy (the pun is Miss O'Connor's) automobile. This is a comic scene but, since the truly absurd is unfailingly touching, it is also both compassionate and affecting. For all that, Enoch is so much of a grotesque any sympathy one feels for his loneliness and love starvation (are Enoch's needs "human" needs?) is vitiated by repulsion toward him. Enoch's spiritual deformity is not profound enough finally to involve us in its consequences; even when we pity him we feel exempted from his plight. The butt of existence, Enoch is humiliated still further. His emotional striptease offends his warm-handed "friend."

The star leaned slightly forward and a change came in his eyes: an ugly pair of human ones moved closer and squinted at Enoch from behind the celluloid pair. "You go to hell," a surly voice inside the ape-suit said, low but distinctly, and the hand was jerked away. [p. 182]

Though humiliated, Enoch is not disillusioned, he is still sure that he can change his condition through the potency of the "new jesus." His dream goal is the *reductio ad absurdum* of the American success myth: he wants to be "THE young man of the future," that is, a gorilla-man. Following the dictates of some compulsive primordial urge—Enoch has a mystic faith in the wisdom of his blood—the repulsive boy kills the man in the gorilla and becomes him, reborn in innocence and stardom. In a real sense, Enoch does, as he had dreamed, better his condition. He achieves at last identity and status. The comic ritual of his rebirth is a parody of the redemption:

Burying his clothes was not a symbol to him of burying his former self; he only knew he wouldn't need them anymore. . . . No gorilla in existence, whether in the jungles of Africa or California, or in New York City in the finest apartment in the world, was happier at the moment than this one whose god had finally rewarded it. [p. 198]

Enoch is reborn in the image of his creature-god. Yet his change of life is illusory; when as gorilla he approaches a man and woman in the park, rather than admire him and shake his hand as befitting a celebrity, they run from him. He is, as before, as always, lonely and despised.

Hazel's killing of his impersonator Solace Layfield parallels Enoch's murder of the gorilla star; they are both, in a sense, self-murders; moreover, both acts are impelled by the influence of the shrunken mummy. As Enoch has been humiliated by the man-gorilla, Haze has been inadvertently mocked by his double, a paid dupe of the spiritual con man Hoover Shoats. (That Hoover is able to unearth Haze's identical double, wearing the same shiny, electric blue suit, driving the same "high-rat colored car," indicates to some extent the gratuitous laws of probability that govern Miss O'Connor's world.) However, Haze kills his double not for mimicking him but for saying that he doesn't believe in Jesus when he really does. That is, Haze runs over the imitation preacher for committing Haze's own heresy. (" 'You ain't true,' Haze said. 'You believe in Jesus.' ") Haze forces his double to strip off his clothes—the clothes of his false life; then Haze runs him down. (Enoch too had stripped off his clothes before entering his new identity.) Before the false prophet (peeled like a potato from the hawker's machine—a recurrent symbolic image) dies, he confesses his sins to Hazel, a captive priest, ministering, in a sense, his own last rites. The confession, which is in effect an objectification of Haze's confession, is one of the few deeply moving scenes in the novel. This is Haze's first revelation of the horror of his own damned soul, his own unadmitted evil. When the double, suffering with guilt and pain, prays to Jesus for help, Haze slaps him on the back (as a doctor does a newborn infant to bring it to life) stopping his breath. The act is an ambivalent one: is Haze putting Solace out of his misery (sending him to eternal life) or is he merely killing him to end his own discomfiture as spectator? To a certain extent both motives are resident in the slap as in any mercy killing. Miss O'Connor leaves the scene deliberately ambiguous.

His double's confession is the turning point in the novel for Hazel. He is aware for the first time that he has sinned, that he is guilty of fornication, blasphemy, murder, and in implication, suicide. The moment of recognition sets in motion the possibility of his salvation; thereafter Haze moves from guilt to mortification to redemption. As Haze is Solace's unwitting redeemer (he punishes Solace for his sins and hears his confession), Solace's confession makes possible Haze's redemption. Having killed his alter ego and redeemed him into innocence, Haze is prepared to start a new life, though its direction is still unclear to him.

Hazel's decayed car, an old Essex which holds neither oil nor water nor gas, is the symbolic vestment of his corrupt existence. On several occasions in the novel Hazel asserts that the car (a "good" car he mistakenly believes) is his substitute for Jesus. Earlier, when Sabbath tells him that her father blinded himself for justification from Jesus, Hazel tells her self-righteously that "nobody with a good car needs to be justified." Hazel's "good car" is his home, his pulpit, and his chance to escape to a new city, all in one. His complete confidence in and reliance on the potency of a defective machine is the blind illusion that sustains him in his spiritual deformity. The car is his sanctuary—his unfailing protector from Judgment. Once the car is destroyed (a policeman pushes it off a cliff, declaring it "not a car"), Hazel's way of life, his defense against Jesus, is destroyed with it. The destruction of the car leaves Hazel unprotected, face-to-face with the universe he has mocked, alone with the awful recognition of his sins. The vulnerability of his machine-womb effects Hazel's final disillusion in the Church Without Christ. There is no longer any material impediment preventing his recognition of Jesus. Looking over the embankment at the washed-out red clay and his disemboweled car, Haze has an epiphany; he sees beyond the visage of evil, the ugly veil masking the real world, to the sight of limitless space—a manifestation of the infinite:

Haze stood for a few minutes, looking over the scene. His face seemed to reflect the entire distance across the clearing and on beyond, the entire distance that extended from his eyes to the blank gray sky that went on, depth after depth, into space. His knees bent under him and he sat down on the edge of the embankment with his feet hanging over. [p. 209]

Hazel's vision is his first and last. It is, in effect, all inclusive; having seen it, he has nothing left to see. The terrible self-awareness that his sight imposes is, like that of Oedipus, unbearable to him. The car is the vestment of his other life, and with its death, Hazel is reborn. He is able then, as Hawks was not, to burn out his eyes to justify his belief in the Redemption. Moreover, Hazel blinds himself because sight, the continuous recognition of his own evil, is no longer tolerable. As penance for his sins, for all sins, he retains intact his last terrible vision into the valley of hell and beyond, into endless space (the awesome province of God). The classical (and Biblical) irony obtains: when Hazel had eyes he saw not, in blindness he achieves at least spiritual sight.

Hazel's blindness is the first in a series of penitential mortifications he inflicts on himself. The only audience to these penances (he does not of course seek any) is his voracious landlady Mrs. Flood, who is in spite of herself finally converted by

the example of Hazel's abnegation and penitence—his sainthood. He eats only enough for the barest sustenance; he lines
his shoes with broken glass and rocks; he wears barbed wire
under his shirt; he exposes himself to cold and illness.

Whereas the religious concern of most of Miss O'Connor's
stories is implicit, resident only in the point of view that informs them, *Wise Blood* is overtly, if unorthodoxly, Catholic.
In a self-contained episode, Hazel's mortification and martyrdom unto death is presented through the witness of his predatory landlady, who is jealous of his suffering because she is
unable to fathom its purpose. Evil and voracious like most of the
characters in Miss O'Connor's world, the landlady is mystified
and consequently angered by Hazel's self-puishment; she feels
cheated, though she regularly steals his money, because she is
unable to possess his motives, to contain in her head the secret
of his behavior. When Mrs. Flood spies on Hazel while he is
sleeping (she devotes her waking hours to the discovery of his
"secret"), she discovers that he has barbed wire wrapped around
his chest:

> "What's that wire around you for? It's not natural," she re-
> peated.
> After a second he began to button the shirt. "It's natural," he
> said.
> "Well, it's not normal. It's like one of them gory stories, it's
> something that people have quit doing—like boiling in oil or being
> a saint or walling up cats. There's no reason for it. People have quit
> doing it."
> "They ain't quit doing it as long as I'm doing it," he said. [p.
> 224]

This is the somewhat shrill thesis of the novel: though the
world is encrusted with evil ("A good man is hard to find"), if
one man is willing to sacrifice himself in Jesus' image, redemption is still possible. Hazel is the fallen Adam (to borrow a
conception from Genesis and R. W. B. Lewis) who achieves at
last a greater innocence than that he had lost, journeying into
the hell of evil and returning, purged, purified, reborn. In implication, Hazel's is a mythic journey, traversing the three
consequential possibilities of man's spiritual condition: Adam,
Satan, and Christ. The journey back from hell is inevitably

more difficult than the Fall. For all but Hazel, Miss O'Connor
suggests, it has become prohibitively difficult. His redemption is
therefore intended as exemplary, that is, it makes possible the
redemption of his world.

When Mrs. Flood presses Hazel for an explanation of his
behavior, he makes his first and only confession. He says, "I'm
not clean." Earlier in the novel, he had protested, though no
one had challenged him, "I am clean. I AM clean." The excessive protest is no less an admission than the explicit confession, with one essential difference: at the end of the novel
Hazel accepts the fact of sin and the existential possibility of
redemption.

Hazel's death passes virtually unnoticed; he is found near-
dead in a drainage ditch by two fat policemen, authority-
representatives of their society, who, out of gratuitous malice,
club him into unconsciousness (his crucifixion). The law
enforcers deliver Hazel's corpse to Mrs. Flood and she at last
has uncontested possession of him. Her verbal fondling of the
crucified saint sugests at first the necrophilia of Faulkner's
Emily. However, Miss O'Connor's purpose is other: Mrs.
Flood's love of the dead man comes not from sexual frustration
but from the spiritual-emotional equivalent; it is an act of
conversion, an act, in the religious sense, of love. She becomes,
like Mary Magdalene, a convert to his example, a disciple to
his sacrifice. Since she is representative of her evil world, she
experiences illumination for all of us. When Mrs. Flood looks
into his burned-out eye sockets, the eyes blinded as an act of
ultimate belief, she discovers his secret. She glimpses beyond
the barrier of life to the God in him, which implies, of course,
the God in herself. She has, through Hazel, a partial illumination of the eternal. Miss O'Connor's description suggests the
miracle of Mrs. Flood's vision:

She leaned closer and closer to his face, looking deep into them
[his eye sockets], trying to see how she had been cheated or what
had cheated her, but she couldn't see anything. She shut her eyes
and saw the pin point of light but so far away that she could not
hold it steady in her mind. She felt as if she were blocked at the
entrance of something. She sat staring with her eyes shut, into his
eyes, and felt as if she had finally got to the beginning of something

she couldn't begin, and she saw him moving farther and farther into the darkness until he was the pin point of light. [p. 232]

Her insight is revelatory (like Hazel she sees for the first time when her eyes are closed). She envisions Hazel, illuminated by God's light, ascending to Him. In a corrupt world, redemption is possible only through an extreme act, an act of absolute, irrevocable sacrifice. Hazel, as grotesque saint, becomes the "new jesus" he has prophesied.

It is all very neatly worked out, but this very neatness is the besetting limitation of Miss O'Connor's fictional world. Her grays finally separate of themselves, as if their component blacks and whites were only temporarily miscible. Her world lacks breadth and texture; it hangs gloomily in space, revolving on its axis, but it manages—and this is its achievement as art—to create its own claustrophobic reality. She has, it is dull to say, a fecund imagination and her conceptions are, for lack of a more scrupulous word, brilliant. Yet, for all that, much of the experience of her fiction is either private or abstractly rendered. That her most potent scenes rely on the impact, comic and pathetic, inherent in the nightmare reality of her situations suggests that the nature of her talent often distorted the explicitly theological concerns that inform her work. The ending of *Wise Blood*, despite its thematic justification, is not wholly convincing as experience. It is certainly less interesting than the comic vision of hell that precedes it. Though Miss O'Connor's world is private, operating for the most part under its own secret laws, it is not wholly exclusive. On occasion it admits our world inside its borders. At times we recognize her world as an intensification of our own, our shadow-world given shape and substance, our evil dreams objectified. This aspect of her fiction relates it to the American gothic of Hawthorne and Faulkner— in particular the Faulkner of *As I Lay Dying*. In another sense, however, her world *is* exclusive. Though it admits of other worlds and other influences, it is unique. She is a less impressive rhetorician than many another southern novelist, but her style, an admixture of the lucidly simple and the baroque, adequately accommodates her vision. Even if we have reservations about the significance of what she did, we must admit that she did it incomparably well. Her best stories, "A Good Man is Hard to Find," "The Artificial Nigger," "The Displaced Person," and *Wise Blood* sear the consciousness with the acid of their vision, burn away the euphemisms and confront us with the absurd nightmare of existence.

Miss O'Connor's world, encrusted by evil, is populated by the physically and spiritually deformed, distorted images of ourselves, whose redemption is possible only, if at all, through an exemplary and violent act of self-sacrifice. Though she permits us to laugh at the nightmare of our moral deformity, it is a painful laugh tortured by the agony of recognition. We are doomed, she is telling us, to the hell of our own souls unless, at the last extremity of suffering, at the risk of everything, we discover the awesome judgment (and love) of God. It is a small and terrifying hope she leaves us. The rest, the life we live, is merely a comedy, a deadly comedy, of horrors.

7 · All Men Are Jews:

The Assistant by Bernard Malamud

"Without heroes, we're all plain people
and don't know how far we can go."
—*The Natural*

"O God that madest this beautiful earth,
when will it be ready to receive thy saints?
How long, O Lord, how long?"
—*Saint Joan*, George Bernard Shaw

1

IT IS a commonplace by now that much of the excitement of
recent American fiction has been generated, at least in part, by
the emergence of an unaccountably large number of gifted
Jewish writers. Saul Bellow, Norman Mailer, Michael Seide,
Herbert Gold, Bruce Jay Friedman, Bernard Malamud, Edward
Lewis Wallant, Philip Roth, Norman Fruchter, Mark Harris,
Grace Paley, J. D. Salinger, to name only those who come immediately to mind, share in a common national and religious
heritage—a common traditional past. For all that, their like-
nesses as writers are less remarkable than their differences. One
cannot view them as a kind of literary school without minimiz-
ing or distorting the concerns of each. To compare Bellow with,
for example, Wouk, as Maxwell Geismar does in *American
Moderns* on the grounds that they are both Jews, is as blatant
an example of critical vulgarity as a *New Yorker* review which
matches Cervantes with Peter de Vries on the grounds that
they share in a common tradition as comic novelists. That a
large number of our contemporary writers happen to be Jewish
is a sociological phenomenon, not a literary one, interesting in
its own right as a source of investigation but not relevant to the
concerns of criticism. What *is* relevant is the similarity of their
moral preoccupations, the concentration on the burden and
ambivalence of assuming personal responsibility in a world
which accommodates evil—a concern shared by many contemporary writers who are not Jewish.

Perhaps more than any of his contemporaries, Bernard Malamud, in his fables of defeated love and failed ambition, has extended the tradition of the American romance novel, has made
the form into something uniquely and significantly his own.
A moral fabler and fantasist, Malamud writes of the conflicting
demands of the inner and outer worlds of his heroes, of the
tremulous private life confronted by a mythic public scene.
Unlike many contemporary writers of allegorical fiction, Malamud is aware that if a novel is to function as novel, it must
deal first of all with human experience. Unashamedly romantic,
Malamud's fiction delineates the broken dreams and private
griefs of the spirit, the needs of the heart, the pain of loss, the
economy of love.

A romantic, Malamud writes of heroes; a realist, he writes
of their defeats. In our serious arts as in our popular sports, we
demand heroes, men who break records, enact our wildest
fantasies, write great novels. And when we discover, as we must,
that our heroes are, after all, fallible, we are disenchanted and
pillory them for having failed us, for not having transcended
our own poor humanity. In crucifying our heroes, we create
after the fact our saints. And this in part is the subject of
Malamud's three novels: *The Natural* (1952), *The Assistant*
(1957), and the last and least, *A New Life* (1961). The rest is
love. Love is the redemptive grace in Malamud's fiction, its
highest good. The defeat of love is its tragedy. Love rejected,
love misplaced, love betrayed, loveless lust: these are the main
evils in Malamud's fictional world, where (in contrast to
Flannery O'Connor's) a good man is not too hard to find. Yet
the world, for all its potential goodness, is not good, and the
good man, the man capable of love, is inevitably the sufferer,
the sacrifice, the saint.

A New Life is to Malamud's career what *The Adventures of
Augie March* on a larger scale was to Bellow's, a breaking away
from the airlessness and intensity of his two earlier novels, an
attempt to extend the range of his concerns beyond the impulse
of his talent. Whereas the worlds of *The Natural* and *The
Assistant* are vaguely indicated, have a kind of mythic place-
lessness, the setting of *A New Life*—Cascadia College in the
Pacific Northwest—is obviously an actual place, transparently

disguised for the sake of fiction. A *New Life* is a new form, a
demi-picaresque in which the hero wanders quixotically through
a series of comic misadventures, all taking place in the provincial
(microscosmic) community of Cascadia College. The hero, S.
Levin, "reformed drunkard" and New Yorker, unreformed romantic, comes West (to the land of innocence) to remake his
life and to teach freshman composition. A typical Malamud
hero, Levin at thirty, has been a failure all his life and the trip
west, the job at Cascadia, constitute a romantic attempt to
reverse the pattern of his fate, to escape the stigma of his past,
to become nothing less than a new man. In the terms of the
novel's melodrama, the instructorship at Cascadia is a first and
last chance for Levin to succeed at "the career of his choice."
Inevitably, he fails; in Malamud's gnomic universe, fate is
irreversible. Yet in the context of the novel, defeat becomes a
triumph: Levin rediscovers in his failure the best of himself,
the lesson of his old life.

Levin discovers himself by discovering what he is not. The
men on the faculty at Cascadia who represent the kind of life
Levin wants ultimately for himself disillusion him in one way
or another, with one curious exception: Duffy, the failure he
has replaced, a man he never meets. The first Levin hears of
his predecessor, "the disagreeable radical" who left Cascadia
"publicly disgraced" is when Gilley, the director of composition,
assigns him Duffy's former office. Later, informing Levin of his
duties, the department chairman (Fairchild) is instinctively
reminded of Duffy and warns the new instructor to avoid the
pathetic fate of his predecessor—"A broken man, the shadow
of himself, quickly abandoned by all." If Levin is to succeed in
his new life, Duffy is absolutely not the man for him to emu-
late, yet Levin is attracted despite himself to the mysterious
circumstances of Duffy's failed career and goes out of his way
to uncover the mystery. Uncompromising with principle and
the needs of the heart, Levin gradually discovers that he has
been following Duffy's life, error-by-error, as though it were the
predestined pattern of his own. Levin uncovers the secret of
Duffy's past by reliving it.

It soon becomes apparent that A *New Life* has two separate
and distinct concerns which, for all of Malamud's matchmak-

ing, never quite come together. As social realism, the novel is a satire on a kind of monolithic land grant college which offers everything its students need except the humanities—the needs of mind and spirit. The satire is occasionally pointed, but even at its best it is second-rate Malamud; and only as plot device is it relevant to the world of Levin's inner life—the real subject of the novel. As psychological fantasy ("romance"), A *New Life* deals mainly with Levin's double search for self and love and his guilt-ridden love affair with Pauline Gilley, the wife of the man who has given him his job. A refugee from the tenements of New York, Levin is romantically enamored of the country, uncannily touched by its beauty and mystery. When in a magical scene Pauline offers herself to Levin in the woods, choosing him as her lover, Malamud's hero achieves momentarily the fulfillment of his romantic quest—the pastoral idyl—which is the ultimate promise in our literature of the trip west: "He was throughout conscious of the marvel of it—in the open forest, nothing less, what triumph!" [1]

Prompted by Pauline's questions about his life, Levin tells her the secret of his past, of how, sick with despair, an alcoholic on the verge of suicide, he had a revelation which convinced him to go on living:

> "But one morning in somebody's filthy cellar, I woke under burlap bags and saw my rotted shoes on a broken chair. They were lit in dim sunlight from a shaft or window. I stared at the chair, it looked like a painting, a thing with a value of its own. . . . Then I thought, Levin, if you were dead there would be no light on your shoes in this cellar. I came to believe what I had often wanted to, that life is holy. I then became a man of principle." [p. 201]

Levin's revelation of the sacredness of life is a discovery of God and, in implication, the discovery (or illusion) of his own sacred destiny as "a man of principle." When he finishes telling about himself, Pauline says cryptically, "I sensed it. I knew who you were." What she means, of course, is not only that Levin corresponds to her dream image of him but that their destinies are interrelated, that Levin has come to Cascadia to be, in some

---

1 Bernard Malamud, A *New Life* (New York: Farrar, Straus & Cudahy, Company, Inc., 1952). All quotations are from this edition.

way, her savior. At this point, Levin is content being merely her lover.

When the affair with Pauline continues, Levin, the "man of principle," becomes aware of the ambivalence of his idyl; in achieving love (a good), Levin is betraying Gilley, a man who had befriended him when he needed a friend. Levin's melodramatic dilemma is clearly defined: what takes priority in a world of isolation, loss, and pain—love or principle? Malamud resolves this conflict by diminishing Gilley out of existence, by making him so totally despicable that Levin's betrayal of him seems no more than just retribution. That Levin wants desperately to succeed in his new career presents a further complication since he knows that if his relationship with Pauline is discovered he will be summarily fired, his career as college professor ended almost before it has begun. To make matters even more difficult for himself, the "man of principle" has quixotically committed himself to fighting for certain needed reforms in the college. Malamud's world is perversely whimsical; it grants boons but tarnishes them in the process; no gain is without loss.

Love is sacred in Malamud's universe; if life is holy, love is a holy of holies. At the end of the novel, Levin achieves a kind of unsought heroism in sacrificing his career for the *principle* of love, a love in itself dormant, a memory beyond feeling. Accepting responsibility for having once been in love with Pauline, Levin agrees to marry her, to take on the burden of her two sickly children, which also means—Gilley's blackmail demand —that he must give up hope of ever teaching in college again. The knowledge of Duffy's death (Duffy also loved Pauline) further influences Levin's decision. In leaving Cascadia with Pauline and her two adopted children, Levin is fulfilling an implicit commitment to Duffy, who has been the example of his behavior. In completing the broken pattern of Duffy's life, Levin redeems his spiritual father's failure. Thus Levin's act of heroism becomes, in another context, an act of love.

The quality of this heroism is defined for us in his last confrontation with Gilley. When as a favor to Pauline, Levin asks her rejected husband for custody of the children, Gilley responds by pointing out to him the prohibitive drawbacks of marrying a chronically discontented woman and of assuming responsibility for a ready-made family. When Levin, against all logic, seems bent on going through with his decision, Gilley is amazed:

"An older woman than yourself and not dependable, plus two adopted kids, no choice of yours, no job or promise of one, and other assorted headaches. Why take that load on yourself?"
"Because I can, you son of a bitch." [p. 360]

A *New Life* is principally about Levin's heroic destiny: his discovery of what it is and his acceptance of what it entails; the other characters, with the possible exception of Pauline (and Gilley at the end), are caricatures and stereotypes, part of the allegorical landscape of Levin's quest. Malamud is at has best in this curiously flawed novel in illuminating the underside of Levin's consciousness, the arena of his dark, hallucinated dreams, of his war with the past and his uneasy peace with the future.

2

Each of the heroes of Malamud's novels undergoes a mythic journey to test the stuff of his heroism. Levin is partly successful; Pauline, barren all her life, is pregnant with his child at the end, a boon of the hero's triumph, the gift of life. However, in the attrition of his guilt-ridden affair with Pauline, Levin looses (at least temporarily) the ability to feel love, his victory diminished by his loss. The least promising of Malamud's heroes, Frank Alpine (*The Assistant*), is the most successful, renewing in his own spiritual rebirth the saintly life of his exemplary father. Conversely, the most gifted of Malamud's heroes, Roy Hobbs (*The Natural*) fails to fulfill his extraordinary potential, compromises with his principles, and is defeated by the retribution of fate. While Levin and Frank are redeemed through the commitment of love, which makes possible their heroism (the momentary transcendence of their mortality), Roy Hobbs is destroyed by false love, compulsively sacrificing his destiny to the desire of the moment—"the expense of spirit in a waste of shame."

The least known of Malamud's work, *The Natural* is a curious combination: a zany baseball story in the tradition of "Alibi Ike" and an allegory about the Grail quest and the plight of the mythic hero in the modern world. The Grail hero, Roy Hobbs (linguistically, king rustic, an analogue of Percival), is a knight of knights, a noble clown, victimized by fate, defeated by circumstances beyond his power to anticipate or control, and yet, in some way, ultimately responsible for the facts of his existence. Hobbs (like Gatsby) is part Grail knight and part absurd, existential hero, whose goal, to be "the greatest in the game," is meaningful only in terms of a perfect (romantic) commitment to an impossible dream.

An over-reacher, Hobbs is struck down by fate for his presumption. On route from somewhere in the Far West (the opposite of Levin's journey) to a tryout in the big city, Roy meets Harriet Bird, a beautiful, mad girl in black ("certainly a snappy goddess"), who seems to have a special interest in great athletes. The girl is cool to Roy until he demonstrates his supernatural ability—his identity as hero. In a two-man game (pitcher against batter) played on the side of the tracks during a mysterious train stop, Roy shows his stuff by striking out on three pitches the American League's leading hitter, Walter "the Whammer" Wambold. As a tribute to Roy's deed and his boast—" 'I bet someday I'll break every record for throwing and hitting' "—Harriet gives him the hero's reward, a silver bullet in the stomach, death to his presumptions:

She pulled the trigger (thrum of bull fiddle). The bullet cut a silver line across the water. He sought with his bare hands to catch it, but it eluded him and, to his horror, bounced into his gut. . . . Fallen on one knee he groped for the bullet, sickened as it moved, and fell over as the forest flew upward, and she, making muted noises of triumph and despair, danced on her toes around the stricken hero.[2]

When in the second part of the novel, Roy Hobbs mysteriously reappears (resurrected) fifteen years after his fatal wound to play for the New York Knights (managed by Pop Fisher), who in a rainless season have lost a record number

2 Bernard Malamud, *The Natural* (New York: Farrar, Straus & Cudahy, Company, Inc., The Noonday Press, 1961), p. 41. All quotations are from this edition.

of games in a row, the scheme of Malamud's allegory becomes clear. Pop Fisher, an analogue of the legendary Fisher King, rules impotently over a cursed and barren team. It is the task of Roy, the potential Grail hero, to redeem Pop and his Knights (to break the "whammy" which has "jinxed the team") by bringing them the pennant. In *The Natural*, baseball superstition is escalated ironically into myth. Roy's first hit, which literally "knocks the cover off the ball," brings as its boon three days of continuous rain, magically ending the drought. Thereafter, the fortunes of the Knights miraculously reverse until they become the best team in the league, all but unbeatable. With the Grail of the pennant in sight, Roy, deceived again by the temptation of false love, fails in his elected task. The past repeats itself and Roy, no Grail knight after all, relives his own destruction.

Malamud's baseball world is fluid and magical—the landscape of a dream. Characters from thé first part of the novel, dead and half-forgotten, reappear in slightly different shapes, giving Roy, as hero *manqué*, the occasion to re-enact the failures of the past. Whammer, Sam, and Harriet in the first part of the novel correspond to Bump, Pop, and Memo Paris in the second. Like the Whammer fifteen years before, Bump is the league's leading hitter when Roy appears. Hearing Bump's voice for the first time ("a strong, rawboned voice, familiar from his boyhood"), Roy is reminded of the Whammer, only to recall that the Whammer had long since retired. It is also, Malamud suggests, the voice of Roy's father, further suggesting that the Whammer and Bump are intended as father-surrogates in the myth of the novel. And Roy, like Oedipus, like all of us, has a predilection for inadvertently slaying his fathers. In striking out the Whammer, Roy destroys the former slugger's confidence, brings an abrupt end to his career ("Dropping the bat, he trotted off to the train, an old man"). Similarly, Roy is indirectly responsible for Bump's death. With his job threatened by Roy's presence on the team—they are both left fielders— Bump, attempting a heroic catch, crashes into the stadium wall, never to regain consciousness. After his death, Roy, "the bumpkin" replaces Bump as left fielder and for a while seems to the fans indistinguishable from his predecessor. Roy asserts his identity, finally, by being better than Bump, by being "the best in the game." The destruction of the father, however, that ultimate identification, is a prophecy of one's own destruction.

Though no one else blames him, Memo Paris, who was Bump's girl, holds Roy responsible for her lover's death. Vulnerable to the temptation of "snappy goddesses," Roy falls in love with the vindictive Memo, the conventional dark lady of myth and fiction. (In case the symbolism is unclear, Malamud lets us know that both Harriet and Memo remind Roy of his actual mother, a fallen woman who ruined his father's life.) Pop Fisher warns Roy of Memo: " 'She is unlucky and always has been and I think there is some kind of whammy in her that carries her luck to other people.' " A chronic victim of misplaced love, Roy, however, is fatally attracted to the personification of his unlucky fate. Inevitably, she brings about his downfall.

As Bump and Memo are counterparts of Whammer and Harriet, Pop Fisher is an avatar of Sam Simpson, the scout who, fifteen years before, had "discovered" Roy. At the time, Sam was bringing the hero to Chicago for a tryout in the hope that Roy's success ("he is more devoted to me than a son") would redeem his own failed career. Instead of saving Sam, Roy is the occasion of his death. Catching for the hero in his duel with the Whammer, Sam is knocked down by the third strike; he dies a few hours later, a victim of his son's lethal fast ball. As spiritual father to Roy, Pop is also dependent on the hero for the renewal of his career. In a weak moment, the manager admits the extent of his fondness for his star player: " 'My boy, if you knew what you meant to me—' 'Don't say it.' Roy's throat was thick with excitement. 'Wait till I get you the pennant' " (p. 127).

The pennant, the Grail of Malamud's allegory, is the ultimate gift of hero to Fisher king (of son to father), the renewal of life. When Roy comes to bat for the last time, with two out in the ninth inning and the tying run on third base, Pop pleads with the hero to "keep us alive." In the context of the novel, the myth grown large, winning the game (and pennant) is a matter of life and death. Though we never actually find out what happens to Pop after the pennant's loss, Roy, in failing, for all intents and purposes, kills the old man.

Like Bellow's Henderson, Roy (a rain king in his own right) *wants* insatiably, which is at once the impulse of his heroism and the final cause of his defeat. A Malamudian hero, Roy is impelled by dreams of a noble future, of love and children, of the pastoral idyl of his childhood, and, at the same time, haunted by the nightmare awareness of their impossibility, of their irrevocable loss. A naïf, he corrupts his ideals by mistaking the occasion of their fulfillment. He rejects Iris Lemon, who loves him, for Memo Paris and gets the American hero's reward— emasculation and defeat. Starved for Memo's love, Roy becomes a voracious eater in compensation. Playing on his weakness for her, the temptress plies the frustrated hero with huge quantities of food, a counterfeit of love (the analogue of Harriet Bird's bullet), until Roy collapses with a colossal bellyache, "a reenactment of the past." With Roy disabled and lost to the team, the Knights lose their remaining three games and the pennant race, all but won, ends in a tie.

His ideal of himself compromised beyond repair, Roy accepts a bribe "to throw" the playoff game in order to win Memo by paying, in a double sense, her price. When the hero decides late in the game that he wants desperately to win ("the most important thing in his life"), it is too late; he is unable to reverse his commitment to Memo. At a crucial point in the game, Wonderboy, Roy's marvelous bat (the symbolic sword of his potency), breaks in two. A further quirk of fate: Roy finds himself confronted in his last at bat by Herman Youngberry, the personification of his lost youth, an avatar of himself of fifteen years ago. The rookie relief pitcher, a twenty-year-old farm boy, strikes the hero out (as Roy had Whammer) on three straight pitches. Replaced by Youngberry, Roy is transformed momentarily from hero to scapegoat—a homiletic illustration of the tenuousness of fame. The hero's career completes its cycle. The baseball commissioner announces that if the rumor of Roy's selling out is true (can Roy even deny it?), "he will be excluded from the game and all his records forever destroyed." This is the ultimate defeat for the natural who had hoped (his dream of greatness) to live eternally in the record of his triumphs. Given the absurd context of the pennant race, Roy's failure is quixotic, a tragic joke on his romantic dreams and, since they are our dreams too, on all of us.

Though the mythic superstructure of Malamud's first novel is unobtrusive, expressed for the most part in felt experience, it seems, by the same token, somewhat gratuitous, a semiprivate literary joke between author and academic reader. *The Natural*, as experience, is a wildly funny, and sad, baseball tale, informed by the fantasy of heroism and the nightmare frustration of defeat. Its pleasure is not in its allegory, though Sir Percival as baseball star is a witty idea, but in the hallucinated and idiomatic particulars of its narrative. Committed to its scheme, *The Natural*, on occasion, seems overplotted; too much is governed by fortuitous circumstances in the guise of fate. At his worst, Malamud has a predilection for manipulating his characters, denying them self-motion, in order to accommodate the antinovelistic demands of his moral allegory. This is his major flaw, the vice of his virtue, and it mars to a lesser extent his brilliant second novel, *The Assistant*, one of the most concentrated and powerful works of fiction to come out of America since the Second World War.

3

The most Dostoevskian of Malamud's novels, *The Assistant* is about an ambivalent saint, a man who in seeking expiation for a crime succeeds only in increasing and intensifying the burden of his guilt. The hero Frank Alpine is congenitally and circumstantially unable to translate his good intentions into moral acts. In the end, however, racked by anguish and suffering, he finds the occasion to redeem his sins, electing to live the saint's life of the old man he has sinned against. *The Assistant* has two central biographies: the life and death of Morris Bober, unwitting saint, and the guilt and retribution of Frank Alpine, saint-elect, the first life creating the pattern and possibility of the second. At the end, as if by metamorphosis, the young Italian thief replaces the old Jewish storekeeper, the reborn son replacing the father.

Morris Bober, the luckless owner of an impoverished grocery store, is the center of the first half of the novel. That he is a

Jew in a non-Jewish area, a commercial failure surrounded by success, an honorable man among thieves, indicates his inescapable isolation—his exemplary role. Early in the novel, in a passage which has a gnarled eloquence, Malamud defines the terms of Bober's existence:

The early November street was dark though night had ended, but the wind, to the grocer's surprise, already clawed. It flung his apron into his face as he bent for the two milk cases at the curb. Morris Bober dragged the heavy boxes to the door, panting. A large brown bag of hard rolls stood in the doorway along with the sour-faced, grayed-haired Polisheh huddled there, who wanted one.
    "What's the matter so late?"
    "Ten after six," said the grocer.
    "Is cold," she complained.
    Turning the key in the lock he let her in. Usually he lugged the milk and lit the gas radiators, but the Polish woman was impatient. Morris poured the bag of rolls into the wire basket on the counter and found an unseeded one for her. Slicing it in halves, he wrapped it in white store paper. She tucked the roll into her cord market bag and left three pennies on the counter.[3]

It is autumn on the calendar but already winter in Bober's world. The writing is empathic, evoking the unrelieved burden of Morris' day-to-day existence. The old Polish woman is seen as Morris sees her, "a sour-faced, gray-haired Polisheh." She has no other identity because she has no other existence in the novel except as one of Morris' private ghosts. The details of his morning, performed every morning for all the waking-suffering days of his life, are ritualistic—attrition enacted by rote. To sell a three-cent roll, he must wake up and go out into the cold an hour earlier than he would otherwise. Though he is an old man and needs his rest more than the three pennies, he feels constrained to serve the dour old Polisheh out of an uncompromising sense of the responsibilities of his office. That he continues to serve her thanklessly despite her chronic discontent is a part of his burden, his anonymous decency in an indecent and abusive world. Like the grocer in Malamud's short story "The Bill," Morris, despite his practical resolves, extends credit indiscriminately, even in cases where he knows payment is un-

3 Bernard Malamud, *The Assistant* (New York: New American Library, 1958), p. 7. All quotations are from this edition.

imaginable. If it is in his power to satisfy them, he will not ignore the needs of another human being. It is the least one man can do for another. He is, therefore, an easy mark, a victim of his own undiscriminating kindness. Like Roy Hobbs, he does not learn from the past; he continues to believe human beings are better than their actions; he continues, in spite of all the evidence of his suffering, to extend the grace of trust. Before the action of the novel begins, he has been thoroughly cheated by a man whom he has trusted as his partner; he has had his livelihood diminished by his "friend" Karp who rents a store across the way to a rival grocer. His victimization is not limited to man's inhumanity but is compounded by the fates; he is a predestined, inexorable sufferer. His daughter Helen, who is a sufferer in her own right, contrasts her father's low estate to that of his successful neighbor Karp:

The grocer, on the other hand, had never altered his fortune, unless degrees of poverty meant alteration, for luck and he were, if not natural enemies, not good friends. He labored long hours, was the soul of honesty—he could not escape his honesty, it was bedrock; to cheat would cause an explosion in him, yet he trusted cheaters—coveted nobody's nothing and always got poorer. The harder he worked—his toil was a form of devouring time—the less he seemed to have. He was Morris Bober and could be nobody more fortunate. With that name you had no sense of property, as if it were in your blood and history not to possess, or if by some miracle to own something, to do so on the verge of loss. At the end you were sixty and had less than at thirty. It was, she thought, surely a talent. [p. 17]

Karp's luck, as if parasitic, seems to improve only when someone else's (usually Morris') gets worse. If Karp has a golden touch, Morris has a leaden one, the two like counterweights on a universal balance. When two men come to hold up Karp's plush liquor store, they end up (as Morris' "talent" would have it) robbing and beating the impoverished grocer. Morris accepts even this unutterable indignity, as he has the long line of lesser ones preceding and anticipating it, with hopeless resignation and a sense of renewed guilt for his failure. As he sees the gun irrevocably descend, Morris

felt sick of himself, of soured expectations, endless frustration, the years gone up in smoke, he could not begin to count how many.

He had hoped for much in America and got little. And because of him Helen and Ida had less. He had defrauded them, he and the bloodsucking store.

He fell without a cry. The end fitted the day. It was his luck, others had better. [p. 25]

Morris, even on the verge of destruction, has faith in God's justice, accepts the responsibility for his lot. Though he continues to suffer until death brings him relief, after the robbery he is no longer the center of the novel's focus; he is replaced by Frank Alpine, one of the men who robbed his store. The old grocer's Jobean existence defined early in the novel provides an anticipatory parallel and exemplar to Frank's penitential suffering and final conversion to Judaism.

I suggested earlier the significance of the symbolic father-son conjunction between Morris and Frank—Jew and non-Jew. There are four pairs of fathers and sons dealt with in the novel, Detective Minogue and Ward, Julius Karp and Louis, Sam Pearl and Nat, Morris and Frank; in each the son inherits and fulfills the possibilities of the father. Detective Minogue's merciless rigidity, his inability to give love or pity, make his son Ward into a viciously degraded criminal. When Minogue discovers that Ward has broken into Karp's liquor store, the policeman hunts him down and beats him viciously, with the malice of his own failed responsibility. Ward dies some hours afterward, trapped in a fire from which he is too enfeebled to escape; his father's beating, in effect, is the cause of his death. Earlier in the novel, Minogue, nominally investigating the daily pilfering of a quart of milk and two rolls from the front of Morris' store, asks the grocer if he would recognize Ward if he saw him:

"I don't know," said Morris. "Maybe yes or maybe no. I didn't see him for years."

"If I ever meet up with him," said the detective, "I might bring him into you for identification."

"What for?"

"I don't know myself—just for possible identification." [p. 42]

The detective knows, if only by knowing his own impulses, that his son is the enemy, his enemy and consequently society's. Ward commits crimes—only in his father's area of authority—

seeking punishment, the only recognition his father can give him. That the father has to have a stranger "identify" his son ironically suggests the extent of Minogue's spiritual blindness. The ironic parallels in the scene are extensive. Morris, whose own son has died, pities the detective for having the burden of a son he is unable to recognize. Yet Frank, whom Morris later in a sense adopts as a son, permitting him to work in the family grocery without pay, is the very thief the grocer has been hunting. When Frank disillusions Morris, the universally forgiving grocer is unable to forgive him. Morris has become too fond of Frank to risk further ill use at his hands. The failure of the boy to live up to Morris' ideal of him results in the final disillusionment of the old man; in him, as Malamud puts it in one of his short stories, "breaks what breaks." Blinded by the maze of deceit and ingratitude he has suffered all his life, Morris misjudges Frank, banishes him from the store for stealing when Frank, attempting to undo his wrong, has actually been putting his own money in the cash register. In a sense, Morris, like the detective, becomes unable to recognize his own son.

Frank Alpine, the gentile-Jew, the victimizer and victim, is, until the end of the novel, a mass of internal ambivalences. Despite his intense (actually religious) desire to do good, he is unable to resist the least admirable of his instincts. Out of acquiescence, he accompanies the degraded Ward Minogue when he robs "the Jew's" grocery store. Guilt-ridden for his complicity in Ward's vicious treatment of the grocer, he haunts the area of Morris' store, looking for an opportunity to redeem himself. He makes the occasion, insinuating himself as Morris' assistant without pay. Not only does he run the store for Morris while the injured grocer recuperates but he manages through a conspiracy of salesmanship and circumstance to increase the grocer's income. Disturbed by his own apparent selflessness (a loss of identity), Frank begins to steal small amounts from the grocer—negating one impulse by the other. He is not bad; it is only that he finds it prohibitively difficult to be as good as he would wish—a saint's good. This is the essential paradox of Frank's existence; he means to do good, yet he compulsively continues to do harm. Early in the novel, before we really know

Frank, Malamud introduces us to his romantic admiration for St. Francis, whose pattern of life Frank unsuccessfully imitates. Over a cup of coffee, he passionately explains the saint's concerns to the indifferent candy store owner Sam Pearl.

"For instance, he gave everything away that he owned, every cent, all his clothes off his back. He enjoyed to be poor. He said poverty was a queen and he loved her like she was a beautiful woman."
Sam shook his head. "It ain't beautiful, kiddo. To be poor is dirty work."
. . . .
"Everytime I read about somebody like him I get a feeling inside of me I have to fight to keep from crying. He was born good, which is a talent if you have it." [p. 28]

Like Saint Francis, Morris has a talent for goodness, and in the grocer's abiding gentleness of spirit Frank senses an essential likeness to his patron saint. Though Frank's devotion to Saint Francis as fable is wholehearted, he is ambivalent toward the same qualities in the here-and-now impoverished and suffering grocer: ("His pity leaks out of his pants, he thought, but he would get used to it.") Though repelled by Morris' indiscriminate compassion, Frank is attracted to the grocer's martyred existence. His motive for staying on to help the old man long after his debt of conscience has been repaid is to discover the mystery of Morris' virtue. He feels that the fact of Morris' Jewishness has something to do with the grocer's capacity for self-immolation. Frank asks Morris:

"What I like to know is what is a Jew anyway?"
Because he was ashamed of his meager education Morris was never comfortable with such questions, yet he felt he must answer.
"My father used to say to be a Jew all you need is a good heart."
[p. 99]

Pressed by Frank, Morris insists that it is the following of the Law, the Torah, which makes a Jew. A poor but bountiful man, Morris offers what little information he has. The Law, he tells the boy

"means to do what is right, to be honest, to be good. This means to other people. Our life is hard enough. Why should we hurt somebody else? For everybody should be the best, not only for you or me. We ain't animals. This is why we need the Law. This is what a Jew believes." [p. 99]

Frank's quest is not so easily ended. In the terms in which
Morris has defined Jewish law he recognizes the Christian
doctrine which was taught him as a child. Yet there is a real
difference between Jew and non-Jew which Frank has noticed,
and he pursues his spiritual quest into a moment of imperfectly
shared discovery:

"But tell me why is it that the Jews suffer so damn much, Morris?
It seems to me they like to suffer, don't they?"
"Do you like to suffer? They suffer because they are Jews."
"That's what I mean, they suffer more than they have to."
"If you live, you suffer. Some people suffer more, but not because
they want. But I think if a Jew don't suffer for the Law, he will
suffer for nothing."
"What do you suffer for, Morris?" Frank said.
"I suffer for you," Morris said calmly.
Frank laid his knife down on the table. His mouth ached. "What
do you mean?"
"I mean you suffer for me." [pp. 99–100]

What Morris means, of course, is that one man suffers for
another, yet with a prophet's instinct, he defines the nature and
consequence of his association with Frank. At the end of the
novel (after Morris' death), Frank becomes a Jew, not out of
religious conviction but because he elects to be like Morris, a
good man; he elects to suffer for Morris, who has suffered, and
in a sense died, for him.

Frank's relationship to Morris is as significant to the development of the novel's theme as his unfulfilled love affair
with Helen is to the development of its melodramatic action.
Frank's attraction to Helen is an uneasy fusion of the sensual
and the spiritual: at one moment he rages with lust for her; at
another, he is filled with profound tenderness for her suffering.
Yet even after he comes to know her, she remains unreal to him,
a personification of the beauty of the world from which the
conditions of existence have shut him off. Since he believes that
this beauty is justifiably inaccessible to him, he compulsively
destroys the relationship at the very moment its realization becomes possible. While they are still strangers, Frank's un-
requited desire for Helen impels him to climb an elevator shaft
to spy on her in the bathroom, to make love to her inaccessible
nakedness with his desperate eyes. In a powerful scene, an

evocation worthy of Dostoevsky, Malamud describes the self-induced torments of Frank's shame:

Holding his breath, he crouched motionless, clinging to the swaying ropes. Then the bathroom window was shut with a bang. For a while he couldn't move, the strength gone out of him. He thought he might lose his grip and fall, and he thought of her opening the bathroom window and seeing him lying at the bottom of the shaft in a broken, filthy heap.

It was a mistake to do it, he thought.

But she might be in the shower before he could get a look at her, so, trembling, he began to pull himself up. In a few minutes he was straddling the ledge, holding onto the ropes to steady himself yet keep his full weight off the wood. . . .

He felt a throb of pain at her nakedness, an overwhelming desire to love her, at the same time an awareness of loss, of never having had what he wanted most, and other such memories he didn't care to recall.

Her body was young, soft, lovely, the breasts like small birds in flight, her ass like a flower. Yet it was a lonely body in spite of its lovely form, lonelier. Bodies are lonely, he thought, but in bed she wouldn't be. She seemed realer to him now than she had been, revealed without clothes, personal, possible. He felt greedy as he gazed, all eyes at a banquet, hungry so long as he must look. But in looking he was forcing her out of reach, making her into a thing only of his seeing, her eyes reflecting his sins, rotten past, spoiled ideals, his passion poisoned by his shame. [pp. 61–62]

This scene, in which Frank symbolically violates Helen, anticipates his actual violation of her later in the novel. The same self-destructive instinct that permits the first act compels the second. Frank peeps through the bathroom window, not so much to gratify his lusts as to torture himself with the impossibility of their fulfillment. It is at least partly an act of debasement and self-punishment.

All of the sons in the novel, Nat Pearl, Louis Karp, Ward Minogue, and Frank Alpine, court Helen's love in one way or another. Helen, the least convincing of Malamud's characters, is both practical and idealistic, less ordinary than her surroundings though not extraordinary enough to surmount them. Her dream of bettering herself is an admixture of Bovarism and genuine sensitivity. What she wants, as she puts it, is "the return of her possibilities," though she is only vaguely aware of what her possibilities include. While the unambitious liquor clerk Louis Karp is not good enough for her, she is more than willing to settle for the equally shallow Nat Pearl, an ambitious law student who has apparently risen above his surroundings. It is part of her tragedy that the real Nat is not the dream hero she has romantically envisioned. Insensitive to her, he devalues the gift of her love, taking it as his due, and irreparably wounds the giver. Despite the difference in their situations, Nat is the spiritual heir of his father, a good but materialistic man, whose livelihood comes from selling penny candy. That Helen's dream of a better life might be satisfied by marriage to Nat Pearl suggests the inadequacy of her aspirations. Whereas she loses the possibility of marrying Nat by yielding herself too readily, she loses the possibility of a real relationship with Frank by withholding herself too long. Inhibited by the pain of the first experience, she is unwilling to risk the second until her last nagging self-doubt is assuaged. When Helen is finally sure that she loves Frank, it has become, for a conspiracy of reasons, too late.

Melodramatic circumstances (fate as authorial prerogative) conspire against the ill-fated lovers. While Helen is waiting for Frank in the park to tell him that she loves him, Ward Minogue, also looking for Frank, appears in his place and attempts to rape her. When, after saving her from Ward, Frank forcibly makes love to her, she feels disgraced, as if Ward had actually consummated his attempt; in the merging of the acts, the two identities seem as one. Though circumstances contrive against them, Helen and Frank are in themselves responsible (fate as character) for the failure of their relationship. A Malamudian irony: Helen is able to love Frank only until he makes love to her; the fact debauches the illusion.

Having lost Helen through his lust, Frank, waking from a guilt-ridden nightmare, has a revelation about himself:

Frank got up to run but he had run everywhere. There was no place left to escape to. The room shrank. The bed was flying up at him. He felt trapped—sick, wanted to cry but couldn't. He planned to kill himself, at the same minute had a terrifying insight: that all the while he was acting like he wasn't, he was really a man of stern morality. [p. 139]

Like S. Levin, Frank discovers (in a comparable illumination) that he is a man of principle, but unlike Levin, he is at the same time a compulsive sinner. His own most merciless judge, Frank continually sets up occasions in which he can test his actual self against his ideal of himself. Guilty of imperfection (the presumption of the romantic hero), he debases himself as penance; he destroys his relationship with Helen and continues to steal gratuitously from the grocery store. Since he wants more than anything else to be a good man, his crimes are a means of self-punishment; each time he pockets money from Morris' register, he torments himself with guilt. Moreover, he increases his debt, psychologically and financially, to the grocer, which means he must punish himself still further to make requital. As penitent he must fall deeper and deeper into his interior hell before he can allow himself salvation. This is the pattern of his life and a central concern of the novel.

Malamud uses the changing of the seasons and the seasons themselves as physical symbols, providing his timeless and placeless New York landscape with a kind of metaphysical climate. The novel starts in early November and ends in mid-April, symbolically covering the Fall, the Death, and the Redemption of Man. The seasons mirror the inner condition of the central characters. Winter is the longest season in Malamud's bleak world. Throughout the almost endless winter, Frank, Morris, and Helen suffer their wounds in isolation, waiting for the spring as if it were some sort of relief-bringing god. The February day on which Helen decides to accept Frank's love is a warm, prematurely spring day which carries with it an illusory sense of flowering, of awakened love. She discovers, however, after her nightmarish experience in the park, that she has been victimized by her romantic illusions, that it is still winter, the season of death, the destroyer of love.

Morris too is destroyed by the conspiracy of a protracted winter and an illusory spring. Winter reasserts itself late in March with a heavy snowfall. Morris, refusing to acknowledge the winter cold ("tempting fate"), goes out to shovel snow without a coat. As a direct consequence ("every move he made seemed to turn into an inevitable thing"), he gets pneumonia and dies. Among the ravages of a protracted winter, Morris' death, like his life, goes unnoticed, soundless as the falling of the snow which covers the path he has sacrificed his life to clear. Yet spring ultimately does come, and with its coming Frank, almost triumphantly, renews Morris' existence.

At Morris' burial, Helen tosses a rose into the grave and Frank falls in after it, landing feet first on the coffin. It is an absurd accident, embarrassing the solemnity of the occasion; yet it is also a kind of spiritual communion between son and father. In entering the grave, Frank achieves final identification with Morris, which is the ultimate act of self-sacrifice. His rising from the grave as Morris is a symbolic resurrection; the season aptly enough is spring, shortly before Passover and Easter.

Ironically, Frank's rebirth leads him only to the assumption of Morris' living death in the tomb of the grocery store. In a hauntingly bitter passage, Ida and Helen console each other: " 'Your father is better off dead,' said Ida.

As they toiled up the stairs they heard the dull cling of the register in the store and knew the grocer was the one who had danced on the grocer's coffin" [p. 182].

Like Morris, Frank becomes wholly committed to the store, sacrificing his energies to support Ida and Helen. Totally committed, he even gets up an hour earlier, as Morris had, to sell the three-cent roll to the "Polisheh." In continuing Morris' life, Frank fulfills the possibilities of the grocer's actual son, the son who died while still a child. (Symbolically, the son becomes the father, continues his life by continuing his identity.) It is the least Frank can do for the man he has wronged, and the most. In suffering for Morris and, in Morris' role for all of us, Frank achieves his own redemption, becoming at last a wholly honest and good man. In Frank's purification through pain and suffering, Malamud unites the disparate concerns of mythic ritual and conventional realism. *The Assistant* ends on a transcendent note. As a consequence of Morris' death, Frank finds the occasion to fulfill his no longer self-conscious quest for sainthood.

Frank's redemption is made possible by his uncompromising love for Helen, which provides the impetus of his commitment to the store. A similar commitment is made by the shoemaker's assistant in Malamud's tender short story "The First Seven Years." In the beautiful ending to that story, we get an illumination of the informing spirit of the novel and, as such, the romantic impulse at the heart of all of Malamud's fiction: "But the next morning, when the shoemaker arrived, heavy-hearted, to open the store, he saw he needn't have come, for his assistant was already seated at the last, pounding leather for his love."

The amount of love a man is able and willing to commit to life is, in Malamud's universe, the measure of his grace.

8 · Paradise Lost:

Lie Down in Darkness by William Styron

> Son, you don't have to be a campfollower of
> reaction but always remember where you
> came from. The ground is bloody and full
> of guilt where you were born and you must
> tread a long, narrow path toward your
> destiny.

THIS MYTHIC, almost absurd voice of· Milton Loftis's father,
comes as an echo from Tiresias, chanting in oracular rhetoric
the ritual theme of *Lie Down in Darkness* (1951)—sin and
guilt, guilt and death. These are the trinitarian fruits of the fall.
Port Warwick, Virginia, the soil of William Styron's first novel,
is a decayed and decaying paradise, haunted by illusions of a
glorious past. With the progressive deterioration of its romantic
ideals, the aristocracy of Styron's South falls from innocence
into decay, from decay into guilt, and finally from guilt into
redemption through death. This theme, though recurrent in
southern fiction, has been inherited intact, along with some
characters and episodes, from William Faulkner's *The Sound
and the Fury*. Nor is that Styron's only literary debt. The style
of *Lie Down in Darkness*, studded with jewels of rhetoric, indicates Styron's acquaintance with the writing of at least
Faulkner, Warren, Fitzgerald, Wolfe, and Joyce. However,
given its weaknesses, its often unassimilated indebtedness, its
self-insistent verbal virtuosity, its final failure to achieve focus,
Lie Down in Darkness remains the most ostentatiously talented
first novel of the period. The prodigious brilliance of its performance resides in the richness and grace of the language and
the intricate, almost impossible complexity of the structure.

The plot structure of *Lie Down in Darkness* has all the aspects of a puzzle—a methodic search through a maze of mirrors
for a truth hidden in its symbolic reflection. But as a puzzle it
is never intentionally obscure. We are given at the outset the

first clue: the fact of Peyton Loftis' suicide, a symbol of the final disintegration of the Loftis family. The novel on its narrative level, then, becomes an investigation of the events leading up to Peyton's death, in effect an intensive exploration of a southern family's almost effortless self-destruction. On its symbolic level, *Lie Down in Darkness* is a tragedy of decaying values, a study of a paradise fallen into chaos, the end result of a romantic conception of morality. This is a morality corroded with paradoxes: purity and original sin, chivalry and slavery, innocence and decadence. The social order of the southern slavocracy is long dead, but the dream of glory persists—an idiot ghost haunting its descendants.

The entire forward progression of the novel takes place in less than three hours, a stunning self-imposed limitation. The time present of the novel is the burial of Peyton, a ritualistic symbol of the completion of the life cycle—a going back at last to the starting point of existence. It is no accident that the final scene in *Lie Down in Darkness* is a baptism, a symbol of the renewal of life. The technical problem of exposition that Styron has set himself is Ibsenic: [1] he must move backward and forward in time simultaneously; he must delay revelation of the past so that each discovery further illuminates our understanding of the present, the final discovery, the lifting of the veil, illuminating all. To effect his intention, Styron employs five narrators (six including the author) who reconstruct the significant events of the past that are connected with the final tragedy. Each of the narrators is equipped with the faculty of complete recall and, in some cases, a God-like intuition, which might be considered a kind of cheating on Styron's part. However, the stylized use of internal monologue is a schematic device employed with reasonable consistency throughout.

Milton Loftis, who is the fixed center of a destructive three-cornered relationship, standing uneasily between his daughter Peyton, and his wife Helen, is the first mind through which the narrative (past and present) is filtered. It is a mind dulled by alcohol, guilt, and indulgence. Milton seeks in the storehouse of remembered experience to discover where he failed Peyton,

1 Notably Ibsen's mastery of retrospective exposition influenced the narrative technique of James's later novels.

what particular moment, what action (if he could but undo it!) triggered Peyton's destruction. At first he finds no answer, but he feels that somewhere in his weakness, in his sins, in the sins of his tradition, he is responsible. Unable to live with the knowledge of his guilt, Milton succors himself in the narcosis of drink, looking not for expiation but only painlessness.

Milton, as seen through the eyes of Dolly Bonner who loves him but who is not loved in return, whose body is used by him as another anesthetic against the pain of memory, is a man whose charm of personality would make him most likely to succeed in his chosen field, law or politics. But Milton has already sold this possibility of personal achievement along with his manhood to Helen, for the price of comfort. His failure to realize his latent potentialities is not tragic but pathetic. Pampered by self-delusion, the habit of his traditional past, he is a romantic without romance. He must live in the idealized image of himself even though the picture never comes into focus for him. His obsessive, drunken search for his beautiful daughter Peyton, at a football game, while Maudie, his crippled, idiot daughter lies dying in a hospital nearby symbolizes the fruitlessness of his activity, the nightmare of his failure. Styron makes this graphic for us by having the inebriated Milton carry in his arms a Confederate flag, "a trophy without honor." Milton is good but lost, well meaning but irresponsible—a remnant of a tradition that did not require responsibility.

Milton's romantic yearning, unrewarded in Helen, grows into his incestuous attachment for Peyton, a love which becomes obsessive and is, in part, the cause of her destruction and his disintegration. Unable to consummate his attraction to his daughter, Milton drifts into an extended affair with the vulgar but sexual Dolly Bonner, which, Styron suggests, is a kind of vicarious incest. "Poor blind Milton," says Peyton in a moment of ironic revelation, and this is, in implication, his epitaph. But at Peyton's wedding reception, the nightmarish climax of the novel, Milton does achieve his moment of realization.

Across the room he sees Peyton break away from the young lieutenant, her arm crooked at the elbow in a curious disjointed way. . . . He wishes to go to her side, to talk to her alone, and explain. He wants only to be able to say: forgive me, forgive all of us.

Forgive your mother too. She saw, but she just couldn't understand. It's my fault. Forgive me for loving you so.

But at this moment, when he suddenly sees Helen, white with fury, throw a coat over her shoulders and go out onto the porch with Carey Carr, he knows that explanations are years too late. If he himself could love too much only Helen could love so little.[2]

In a moment of pure unillusioned sight, Milton becomes aware of the irremediable nature of their three-personed tragedy. His discovery, however, only intensifies his helplessness, and so he drinks to forget; soon all that remains of his vision is a blurred sense of discomfort, a vague prescience of undefined and undefinable danger. Nevertheless, this has been Milton's first admission of his excessive love for Peyton, which has, in part, created Helen's obsessive jealousy of her daughter—her devout, self-righteous hate. Helen, Milton, and Peyton are, in effect, like Sartre's trinity in No Exit, one another's inescapable Hell. Under the catalytic influence of the wedding, the thinly disguised pattern of their lives manifests itself: Milton drunkenly mauls Peyton; Helen accuses Peyton of being a slut, of using her sexuality to extort gratuities from her father; Peyton digs her nails into her mother's face. What happens is an intensification of what has been implicit all along; the patina of respectability is torn away, revealing the horror.

Further complicating the process of unraveling the puzzle is the use of narrations within narrations, flashbacks within flashbacks, creating a view of a view of a view—an extended perspective of perception. Styron's technique of indirect narration is most effective when he uses Carey Carr, an acquiescent Episcopal minister, as reporter of the behavior, feelings, and thoughts of Helen Loftis. Carey is Helen's confidant, psychiatrist, father, and spiritual lover all in one. He is a man of love who searches hopefully, but always in vain, for the manifestation of God's goodness in man. A frustrated poet, Carey constructs or rather creates Helen's thoughts and feelings out of the incoherent material of her confidences. His interpretation of her motives is rather overly indulgent at the beginning of their relationship. But he discovers at Peyton's wedding, during

2 William Styron, Lie Down in Darkness (Indianapolis: The Bobbs-Merrill Company, 1951), p. 291. All quotations are from this edition.

which a series of explosive revelations are detonated (a kind of dramatic chain reaction), the ineradicable blackness of Helen's soul. Helen is psychotic, and there is no salvation for her except the escape provided by her madness. She represents for Carey his first confrontation with evil. In a moment of insane revelation, Helen tells him, "Your God is a silly old ass —and my God—my God is the Devil!" The minister, limited by his gentleness of spirit, is unable to cope with the malignancy of Helen's god.

Helen, even in Carey's gracious interpretation of her behavior, is the least sympathetic of the three central characters. Perhaps, because she is an amalgam of two corrupt traditions, the southern and the military, her corruption has been compounded. There is some reference to an unresolved sexual attachment to her martinet father, which might account for her emotional and sexual frigidity. Her fondest memory is of her father in his officer's plumage sitting masterfully atop a silver gelding. The memory image suggests Helen's secret wish to replace her father astride the emasculated horse; in effect, she aspires to dominate and, at least symbolically, emasculate her husband. Helen's justification of her unforgivingness is her pride, the echo of which is reiterated amid the empty ruins of her life. Finally, her pride becomes a masochistic self-indulgence, a persistent picking at a sore.

Using the morally responsible Carey as narrator of Helen's most offensive behavior, Styron stacks the deck against her. She is a victim as well as a murderer, but she becomes so totally despicable by the end of the novel that we are unable to feel pity for her suffering. Helen is incapable of love except a perverted self-love extended to her lame, simple daughter Maudie, the physical personification of Helen's crippled spirit. Helen, like Truman Capote's nether-world inhabitants, can love only "the broken image of herself."

Published when Styron was twenty-six, *Lie Down in Darkness* has some of the zealous faults of young writing. It is at times overwritten; rhetoric occasionally pours forth like unimpeded flood waters, and the structure seems to crumble at the end, perhaps unable to bear the pressure of the style. But these are flaws in an otherwise remarkable book. If Styron's metaphorical language is used indiscriminately at times, it is rarely less than equal to the highest demands of his story. For example, Peyton's fall from grace with Dickie, the first in a long line of compulsive affairs, is evoked by Styron as the Fall, the precipitative moment of her destruction, which is in symbol all our destructions. Her going to bed with Dickie, "whose mind was a sheet of paper upon which no thoughtful word had been written" (p. 342), does not have the romantic justification of passion or tenderness; it is a gratuitous submission. In a sense, this is her first suicide—a moral death that is an endless retribution for her endless guilt. Ivan Karamazov says, "If God is dead, everything is permissible." When Peyton discovers that God, her father, is for all intents and purposes dead, she sins compulsively, committing herself to the implications of a chaotic universe.

Peyton's act of sexual surrender is, in its universal implications, the death of innocence. In the resonance of Styron's prose this becomes a revelation:

The act of love had exhausted them but they slept restlessly, dreaming loveless dreams. The sun rose, began to descend, and afternoon brought a flood of light to the room. The radio, playing faintly from the living room, sent through their dreams a murmurous flow of intrusions: the war, a preacher said, was general throughout the world and at the smoky edge of sleep between wakefulness and dreams, their minds captured words like Christ and anti-Christ only to lose them and to forget, and to stir and dream again.

Sleeping, he took her in his arms; she drew away. A dog barked across the wintry fields. There was dance music and later, Mozart, a song of measureless innocence that echoed among lost ruined temples of peace and brought to their dreams an impossible vision: of a love that outlasted time and dwelt even in the night, beyond reach of death and all the immemorial descending dusks. Then evening came. Arms and legs asprawl, they stirred and turned. Twilight fell over their bodies. They were painted with fire, like those fallen children who live and breathe and soundlessly scream, and whose souls blaze forever. [p. 237]

Peyton is a fallen innocent lost in a world of irreconcilable opposites ("Christ and anti-Christ") which are reconciled for her on the level of ultimate meaninglessness. Her Hell, in which she symbolically burns, is a boundless vale of impossible hopes and irrevocable losses.

In their separate ways Helen, Milton, and Peyton all attempt indulgently to escape the consciousness of guilt; Helen through insanity, Milton through drink and adultery, and Peyton (successfully) through death. Life for Peyton is a football game in which her body takes part and is broken, while her spirit sits like a spectator on the sidelines weeping tears of pity. Where Milton is an idealist without ideals, Peyton is, correspondingly, an innocent without innocence. Loved too much by her father and hated by her mother, beautiful and spoiled, obsessed with death ("how short my time is"), she is a mass of neurotic contradictions. Peyton is aware of her masochistic drives, but she is unable to resist the least of her compulsions. She is without conscious will, and, by divorcing the intent from the act, retains the dream of her innocence. On the borderline of psychosis before her death, Peyton is still able to rationalize her motives:

Oh, I would say, you've never understood me, Harry, that not out of vengeance have I accomplished all my sins but because something has always been close to dying in my soul, and I've sinned only in order to lie down in darkness and find, somewhere in the net of dreams, a new father, a new home. [p. 385]

Peyton regresses at the end to infantilism. Because she cannot find a paternalism on earth to replace the one she has lost, she must go beneath the earth to find "a new father, a new home." Frustrated and lost, she drowns in self-pitying tears as she inexorably lives out the last reel of her phantasmagoric life. She thinks, while climbing a staircase to the height from which she will jump to her death: "I thought that only guilt could deliver me into this ultimate paradox: that all must go down before ascending upward; only we most egregious sinners, to shed our sin in self-destruction, must go upward before the last descent." (p. 385).

Peyton's suicide has all the ritual aspects of a purification. She strips off her clothes (the vestments of her corrupt life) before she jumps, returning to nature in the state of innocence in which she came. Ironically, it is through "falling" that Peyton achieves her redemption. Styron's point is that only through hell —the ultimate Fall—can one finally come to heaven.

Despite the intensity and brilliance of Styron's handling of Peyton's stream-of-consciousness during the moments preceding and leading up to her death, the structure of the novel seems to collapse at this crucial point. Taking place in New York, outside the main setting of the book, Peyton's interior monologue has an alien sound, as if she were another character in another book. Even if the episode in New York can be justified in terms of structure, as necessary for the completion of the puzzle—the final filling-in of all retrospective exposition—it is still inordinately long and dissipates itself as well as the cumulative impact of the novel. Coming as it does after the wedding scene in which her death becomes inevitable, Peyton's state of mind at the moment of suicide seems irrelevant and anticlimactic. Styron tells his story peripherally, in ever-narrowing circles, working toward an ideal, if impossible, center. In attempting to produce that infinite point (that final illuminating) delineating what the novel has already successfully implied, Styron disappoints our expectations. Peyton, by virtue of her complex reality as character, remains finally a mystery.

Symbolism abounds in the over-fertile soil of Styron's novel. Styron evokes the classic myths through transplanting, in a sense, the tragic tradition of the house of Atreus to the marshlands of Port Warwick. I think a fair case can be made for Peyton's being a distant relation of Electra (also Orestes). The flightless birds which follow Peyton to her death are a sort of psychotic manifestation of the furies. Peyton's behavior can be interpreted as a somewhat perverse sublimation of the Electra drive (avenging her father's death by killing her mother in herself). Though the mythic allusions give the novel a further resonance, on occasion symbols seem employed, as in a Tennessee Williams play, merely to create a sort of poetry of atmosphere. One analogy that makes the reader uneasy throughout is that the dropping of the atom bomb on Hiroshima is the national correlative of the central action of the novel. "Don't you realize that the great American commonwealth just snuffed out one hundred thousand innocent lives this week," Harry tells the disoriented Peyton, who a few minutes later jumps to her death. The moral disintegration of the South is a symbol of the disintegration of all of us, and consequently Peyton's suicide is an exemplary act of conscience. The parallel is not wholly invalid, but by over-insisting on it—the bomb is referred to significantly at least a half a dozen times in the novel—Styron makes it seem if not arbitrary, only abstractly relevant.

The ferry ride that separates Port Warwick from the mainland is employed symbolically to suggest the classic voyage across the river Styx into Hades. The fallen paradise of Port Warwick is, like Hades, peopled by the shades of those who once lived:

> The ferry slip is not far form the railroad station, in fact adjoins it, in an atmosphere of coal dust, seedy cafes, run-down, neon-lit drug stores where sailors buy condoms and Sanitubes and occasionally ice-cream cones. The salt-air is strong here. The wind rustles the weeds in vacant lots. Along the railroad track the Negro cabins are lit with the yellow glow of oil lamps, and in the moonlight a black figure appears to pull down the washing. [p. 315]

Port Warwick is a marshland, a quicksand of decay. The landscape acts as a kind of mirror of the spiritual condition of its inhabitants.

> Death was in the air . . . but wasn't Autumn the season of death and all Virginia, a land of dying? In the woods strange, somehow rather marvelous fires were burning across the gray day, the road still shining with last night's rain, gray smoke drifted, bringing to his nostrils the odor of burned wood and leaves. [p. 188]

Virginia is a land of dying, Styron says. But it is a place for degenerative dying. Release, Peyton's fall to death, can only happen outside the narcotic atmosphere of Port Warwick. While Peyton has ended her suffering, Milton and Helen remain, still drowning in the morass of their self-indulgence and self-pity. They are dying too, but slowly, without awareness, engulfed in the sweet-smelling anesthetic of decay.

Harry, Peyton's husband (and father substitute), is used as a symbol of creativeness in contrast to the indolence and self-destruction of Peyton's tradition. Unfortunately, he is unconvincing as a human being and consequently makes a factitious and ineffective symbol. It is ironic that Styron's conceptual representative of life—the New Yorker-Artist-Jew—has less real life as character than his various rotting-on-the-vine southerners. However, the artist as sympathetic character has traditionally been an unaccommodating conception for the writer, who tends to intrude himself, the most sympathetic artist he knows. Mainly, Harry's talk is bad. His literary love making to Peyton ("My blessed Beatrice" [3]) sound like undergraduate self-consciousness. This is in striking contrast to the maturity and control of so much of the writing.

Like Faulkner, Styron also has his symbolic idiot, Maudie. The death of Maudie's innocence, narrated by Helen in a moment of rare understanding, is one of the tragic echoes of the novel. Maudie, crippled and simple-minded, represents another aspect of the southern tradition—its fragile innocence. She retains her innovence until she comes in contact with one of nature's own spirits, Benny [4] (half-Indian, half-Negro), who performs feats of magic to entertain her. He awakens in her the tender wonder of love and she comes each day to meet him, experiencing unalloyed happiness for the first time in her life. But her idyl must finally end; innocence and pure love are merely transient. The death of Maudie's heart comes when she realizes that Benny will leave her, that love does not go on forever. The death of her body follows soon after. What Benny offered her was, after all, only sleight of hand. The symbol of Maudie's disillusionment extends into the following scene in the dramatic sequence of the novel—Peyton's fall from grace with Dickie. They are, essentially, parallel scenes.

The symbol of the southern Negro in *Lie Down in Darkness* as a child in a child's world, who can find salvation through simple faith, has its antecedents in Faulkner's novels. While the southern gentility disintegrates, the descendants of the slave class endure. Ella in *Lie Down in Darkness* and her prototype Dilsey in Faulkner's *The Sound and the Fury* rear the family and try to hold it together, while the family compulsively

3 There is some suggestion that Harry as artist is a kind of symbolic Dante, and his trip to Port Warwick to marry Peyton a descent into purgatory, which may be an excuse, but a poor excuse nevertheless, for his calling Peyton "Beatrice."

4 Faulkner's idiot Benjy was christened Maury and later had his name changed. The names Maudie and Benny suggest the extent that Styron had Faulkner in mind when he wrote *Lie Down in Darkness*.

destroys itself. The source of the Negro's strength is his un-
questioning faith in God, as opposed to the gentry's religion,
which has formalized God out of existence. For all his benevo-
lence and intelligence, Carey Carr is a less effective man of God
than the absurd Negro evangelist Daddy Faith. There are
comparable scenes of religious ecstasy at the end of both (Faulkner's and Styron's) novels. Coming after the burial of Peyton,
the Daddy Faith baptismal ceremony achieves a special resonance as a symbol of the redemption of Peyton's life and of the
possible salvation of our own.

One of the problems of the novel is the paradox of Peyton's
moral responsibility set against the amoral backdrop of Port
Warwick. Is she completely a victim, the end product of a
cursed and decaying southern tradition, or does she have the
possibility of survival? Peyton says in protest against the ir-
responsibility of her parents' generation: " 'They thought they
were lost. They were crazy. They weren't lost. What they were
doing was losing us' " (p. 235). However, through Carey, his
moral raisonneur, Styron holds her responsible—at least in
part responsible. Carey says of Peyton, " 'Other children have
risen above worse difficulties.' " It is this immutable absolute of
judgment, the last standing pillar in a chaotic, disintegrating
society, that gives the novel its final importance.

Though it may fail ultimately, *Lie Down in Darkness* is a
brilliant first novel. Yet our brilliant first novels have been
followed more often than not by a drying up, by a substitution
of will for creation, by second and third novels that fail to go
beyond the promise of the first. It would be pleasant to report
that this does not apply at all to Styron, but to a limited extent
it does. His second book, *The Long March* (1952), a novelette,
though more controlled and concentrated than the first, is
considerably less ambitious; for all Styron's insistences, the
noble defeat of its hero Mannix never quite achieves tragic
dimension. When Styron's second full-length novel, *Set This
House on Fire* (1960), finally appeared, an anticlimax to his
waning reputation, it was inevitably a disappointment. In the
accounting house of our popular criticism, measured against its
ambitions, *Set This House on Fire* is a failure. Yet it is in many
ways an advance over the first novel and it is remarkably better

than the general verdict of its curiously unsympathetic press.

" 'What's the matter with this world?' " a nameless hillbilly singer chants dolefully at a propitious moment in *Set This House on Fire*. The singer, one of Styron's prophetic voices from other rooms, answers his own question: " 'Your soul's on sinking sand, the end is drawing near: That's what's the matter with this world. . . .' " [5]

If anyone still wondered at his point why it had taken the author of *Lie Down in Darkness* eight years to complete his second full-length novel, these lines which inform its experience provide the explanation. Further indicative of Styron's attitude is that all of his sympathetic characters are alcoholics or re-formed alcoholics, as if he were unable to conceive of a sensitive human being who could withstand the nightmare of existence without the anesthetic of drink.

Set This House on Fire attempts the improbable: the alchemi-cal transformation of impotent rage into tragic experience. Styron's rage is the hell-fire heat of the idealist faced by an unredeemably corrupt world, for which he as fallen man feels obsessively and hopelessly guilty. To understand the quality of Styron's anger, one has only to set his protest along side that of the so-called angry young men (Messrs. Braine, Wain, Amis, and Osborne), who seem in comparison nothing so much as choir boys wearing tight shoes. Contemporary man for Styron is an infinitely corruptible Adam, repeatedly violating the terms of his existence, falling farther and farther out of Paradise. Each Adam experiences in the house of his body the torments of a private Hell, the solitary confinement of damnation. The novel contains a series of nightmare visions of Doomsday, at once a prophecy of impending atomic holocaust and an ex-ternalizing of a raging interior guilt. But Doomsday does not so much threaten from without as from within, as Cass Kin-solving, the most central of Styron's three central characters, discovers to his horror and perhaps, final salvation. Cass is, in Styron's over-insistent conception of him, a neo-Dostoevskian hero who goes from the death of sin through the purgation of guilt and suffering to the potential resurrection of redemption.

5 William Styron, *Set This House on Fire* (New York: Random House, Inc., 1960), p. 121. All quotations are from this edition.

It is an exemplary spiritual voyage which Styron suggests makes possible, through the symbolic resurrection of Luciano de Lieto ("like the Phoenix risen from the ashes of his own affliction"), the salvation of all of us damned souls. The novel fails, like the later novels of D. H. Lawrence, because Styron permits his didactic purpose, when it is at odds with his impulses as a novelist, to govern and shape his book. As a result there is often an irreconcilable disparity between the experience resident in the novel and Styron's insistent explication of the experience.

Once we have faced up to the novel's weaknesses—its over-explicitness, its undramatized sermonizing (Styron unabashedly commenting on contemporary civilization through the masks of his sympathetic characters), and its unconvincing "hopeful" ending—we must also, though perhaps with greater difficulty, face up to the fact that *Set This House on Fire* is an original and serious novel which survives, if not wholly transcends, its flaws. Styron's world is a Dantean inferno; he takes us on a descent through levels of disillusioning experiences, some horrifying, some grotesquely comic, in which everything, even what seems most pure, turns out on closer view to be unreclaimably corrupt. Ultimately, the novel is a symbolic pilgrimage into Hell in search of, of all things, the sight of God.

As in *Lie Down in Darkness*, the plot structure is informed by a mystery whose unraveling, we are led to believe, will reveal some essential truth of existence. In both novels, the final discovery is anticlimactic. At the outset of *Set This House on Fire*, we are presented with Peter Leverett, a nondescript Nick Carraway, as first-person narrator and apparently central character. Peter seeks, as the way to his own salvation, the meaning of a nightmare experience in Sambuco, Italy, in which his unholy friend Mason Flagg apparently raped and murdered an Italian servant girl and then killed himself. With the aid of Cass Kinsolving, Mason's antagonist, Peter attempts to reconstruct what actually took place. Along the way, however, the concern of the novel shifts from Peter's quest to Mason as the incarnation of evil (he is, of course, less evil than we had suspected) and then to Cass as a drunken sufferer for an unregenerate world. Cass's chain of self-revelations, through which the mystery is finally uncovered, becomes more significant than the mystery itself. When we actually lift the veil, the secret it has to yield has ceased to be important. Though Cass achieves a kind of redemption through Mason's death, Styron avoids overstating the obvious allegorical parallels. As Mason is not quite Mephisto, and Peter not quite the rock on which the new church is built, Cass is not quite Christ, though these parallels are suggested.

Cass's sleeping nightmares are hardly less real than his waking ones. They are in one way or another recurrent evocations of destruction, sometimes personal, sometimes universal, in which he as southern white, haunted by the guilt of his tradition, is alternately tortured and saved by strangely familiar Negro effigies. Styron's liquid, rhetorical prose, which at times seems to flow on unbidden, is at its best in rendering the nightmare of Cass's hallucinatory visions:

The sea was placid, held in momentary abeyance, but the sun had grown hotter still, hung in the sky fiery, huge and, like some dead weight, oppressively heavy and near. The bugger is exploding, Cass thought as he edged back into a shadowed place, its going to shrivel us like a bunch of gnats in a flame. [p. 483]

There are other, more brilliant passages, but this one suggests both the power of Styron's writing and the central vision of the novel. The swelling sun is a projection of Cass's exploding guilt, but no less a real spectre of contemporary (hydrogen bomb) reality. Despite the philosophical justification for the hopeful ending, this scene and its echoes, and the various parables of corruption and doom that mythically underlie the basic experience of the novel, make the resurrection in the epilogue seem gratuitously appended. The vision of the undying, half-crushed dog offers, I suspect, a more accurate clue to the meaning of Styron's work. Cass witnesses a doctor trying in vain to put the incurably maimed dog out of its misery by beating it on the head with a stick. Although Cass leaves, the vision remains of "the dog's head, mutilated, bleeding, still mouthing its silent, stunned agony to the heavens." The suffering creature, refusing to relinquish its last painful breath to the hand of impotent and brutal mercy, is Styron's metaphor for existence.

Set This House on Fire, a bitter satire on the self-deceit and degeneration of contemporary civilization, a nightmare vision of Doomsday, an allegory of the corruption, death, and redemption of man, does not add up to a complete experience. Although it has its shattering moments, Styron's second novel does not achieve anything like the tragic catharsis of *Crime and Punishment*, which has similar concerns. That its failure can be measured against Dostoevsky's achievement, however, indicates somewhat the quality of its ambitions and the level of its imperfect accomplishment. Like *Lie Down in Darkness, Set This House on Fire*, in its romantic search for truth, a search that in its final implications is perhaps fruitless, in the almost Biblical chronicling of the Fall and Redemption of man, stands without need for apology in the great tradition of the American novel.

9 · The Illusion of Indifference:

The Pawnbroker by Edward Lewis Wallant

> You can hold yourself back from the sufferings of the world: this is something you are free to do and is in accord with your nature, but perhaps precisely this holding back is the only suffering that you might be able to avoid.
>
> —Franz Kafka

> "It's so lonely not to suffer, *so lonely*."
> —*The Children at the Gate*

1

EDWARD LEWIS WALLANT died in 1962 at the age of thirty-six. The four novels which survive him, which will I suspect survive us all, *The Human Season* (1960), *The Pawnbroker* (1961), *The Tenants of Moonbloom* (1963), and *The Children at the Gate* (1964), are dark visions of disquieting, often apocalyptic seriousness, haunting, desolating books about the improbable possibilities of redemption in a corrosively malignant world. Each of Wallant's books is a kind of pilgrim's progress about those blighted innocents, who damned to disbelief, keep vigil at the gate.

Wallant's prose, at its best, seems to brush across the nerve of our feelings in fragile and uncanny ways. Even in his first novel, *The Human Season,* the least successful of the four, there are moments of rending insight, of agonizing perception of character. For example, in a painful confrontation, the benumbed protagonist Berman, overhearing his roomer Russel masturbate, asks "the pathetic stutterer" to move out because he "can't stand to live with someone as miserable as me." Russel tries, impossibly, to defend himself.

"Well, you can thh-hhh-hh-hh-think what you w-want, Mr. Berman, but I certainly w-w-will not burden you w-w—huh huh my huh . . ." His stretched-open mouth revealed the meat sandwich around his tiny, immature teeth. Suddenly his eyes stretched open so wide it seemed the membrane split and they overflowed. He began to make little coughing sounds, which Berman figured to be sobs. Then he began to cry with his eyes open just as wide, gazing with a sort of horror at Berman as though the older man were a grotesque trick mirror that gave him back his image in horrible ugliness.

And Berman sat through it without remonstrance or impatience, feeling he owed himself that much discomfort as some sort of payment. The kitchen was getting dark around the two of them but it was a negligible sort of darkness, a lack of light too trivial compared to that which each of them held in himself. Russel began nodding in time with his sobbing, an agonized sound, as though his soul were shaking itself loose. His thin hands kneaded a piece of the sandwich bread so it seemed the rest of his body was not concerned, was only waiting patiently for the painful sound to end so it could get back to doing some of the feeble exercises its master demanded of it. And Berman, too, was patient, though aging in the melancholy sound of the young man's weeping. He seemed to have put himself several centuries farther from all the life he had lived up till then. He felt almost a sense of drying in his heart and body. He wondered if the remaining hair on his head was losing pigmentation, imagined himself looking in the mirror afterwards to find his hair white, his face creased and ancient.

. . . .

Russel nodded, took a deep breath, and sighed.

"I'll just get my things together."

"No hurry, Russel," Berman said.

"No, I think it would be better if I left as soon as possible under the circumstances. . . ."

Then he must have sensed the tiny smile on Berman's face, for the light was not enough for him to have seen it.

"Why are you smiling, Mr. Berman? Was there something funny?"

"No, just that I never heard you say so much without a single stutter," Berman said.

Russel smiled wryly, yet with a peculiar grace and charm that Berman could see in spite of the darkness.

"There are times with me. . . ."

And Berman nodded in appreciation of the lovely mystery of the phrase, as though at the sight of a long, brief opening which revealed the unrecognizable treasure of the pathetic man.[1]

This scene is in itself as resonant and moving as almost anything in contemporary fiction. And in one guise or another, almost all of Wallant's concerns are here—the profound secretly

[1] Edward Lewis Wallant, *The Human Season* (New York: Harcourt, Brace & World, Inc., 1960), pp. 95–96. All quotations are from this edition.

shared possibilities, tender, awesome, and horrible, of the miraculous fact of being human.

The sharers in Wallant's most powerful novel, *The Pawnbroker*, are the title character Sol Nazerman, a Jew, a survivor of the Nazi camps, and his assistant Jesus Ortiz, a Negro thief—teacher and disciple, surrogate father and son. Their relationship recalls that of Morris Bober and Frank Alpine in *The Assistant*, which may have been one of the sources of its impulse, though *The Pawnbroker* is a considerably darker work. Having come through the blackest extremes of human degradation, Sol Nazerman is at the outset of Wallant's novel, the scar tissue of a man, inured to pain, to love and hate, to the normal shocks of fear, afraid only of the unaccountable ticking of his life. His existence, without pain or pleasure, is a penance to the fact of itself, a monumental attrition. Like all of Wallant's heroes, Sol, in a delicate truce with survival, has of necessity shut himself off from his feelings. He is "sick and dying yet nowhere near the ease of physical death." The novel is about the Pawnbroker's slow return from the carrion sleep of numbness to the agonized awareness of pain, grief, and love—the torturous responsibilities of feeling.

If the Harlem pawnshop is our hell world in microcosm, Sol (the sun) functions in his realm as a kind of merciless god. In extension, then, Sol's grinding despair suggests the hopelessness, the death of possibility of the world; as a consequence, the problem of the Pawnbroker's survival has cosmic implications—the survival of the world, of human life itself, is at issue. Like the grocery store in *The Assistant*, the pawnshop has the sacramental aura of a church, a place of penance and redemption, where Sol and his assistant Jesus dispense with ceremonial judgment, "in exchange for the odd flotsam of people's lives," small loans of cash—the artifact of grace.

For a long time they were busy estimating, haggling, exchanging quick professional signals from time to time. They were a strangely matched team engaged in an even stranger performance, giving mercy with the backs of their hands . . . removing old dreams for the loan of brief new ones, nodding to each other over the innocent heads, negating, winking coldly, holding up fingers in cryptic exchange.[2]

2 Edward Lewis Wallant, *The Pawnbroker* (New York: MacFadden-Bartell, Corp., 1962), p. 81. All quotations are from this edition.

And later when the spiritual winter of indifference that has preserved him in humanlike atrophy begins to thaw:

On and on they came, shy, sullen, sweating, guilty, paying in fear for tiny crimes they had done and were doomed to do, striking out with furtiveness and harshness, sickened with their hereditary curse, weary and ashamed of their small dreams and abandoning the cheap devices they had dreamed with. . . . They packed in one kind of glitter for another, haggled in soft, furtive voices, each ashamed and desperate and hungry, each filling the Pawnbroker's spirit with rage and disgust as he smelled and saw their ugliness.

He stretched on the rack of his sight and smell and hearing, saw all the naked souls ready to spill blood over him. And it began to seem to him that all were making a profit on him, that they found ease from their individual pains at the sight of his great aggregate of pains, that they looked around at the stock of the store and saw it all as a tremendous weight on him. And that seemed to awe them, too, for as they added their own small item it was though they piled on weight to prove his immense power, so that some of them even went out laughing, having left him a piece of their pain. [p. 189]

As Sol assumes the "aggregate of pains" of his customers, Jesus, who patterns himself after the Pawnbroker, becomes an ingenuous conspirator in the strange church-hood of the store. The conspiracy of their relationship, its profane and sacred implications, is at the heart of the novel's experience. Jesus remains in Sol's employ for less actual money than he might earn elsewhere, in the hope of uncovering, as it seems to him, the secret wealth and power of the Pawnbroker's knowledge. For hope of undefined gain, he is Sol's apprentice, a sharer of his burden, though he misconceives until the end the true nature of such an apprenticeship. With an irony too deeply pitched for the boy's comprehension, Sol tells his helper that the only thing in the world he values is money. And so with a disciple's faith, the innocent boy conspires with three other Negroes to rob the Pawnbroker's shop. As Jesus sees it—his own bitter irony—in robbing Sol, he is merely putting into practice the lesson of the master. There are lessons and lessons, however. And at the end, with the instinct of a fit apprentice, Jesus enacts the deepest lesson of Sol's life, reteaches it to the Pawnbroker at the expense of his own. Ultimately, Jesus' sacrifice, a supreme act of faith, moves Sol into reassuming the responsibility of his own feelings, resurrects him from the death of spirit. The death of the son makes possible the salvation of the father.

The excess of contrivance of Wallant's allegory occasionally intrudes, though does not in any significant way deform the deeply perceived flesh and spirit of the novel's experience. The figure of the Pawnbroker looms through the work, a colossus of despair, carrying the burden of the world's horror in the dull pain of his spirit. He is an amazing characterization, one of the memorably dark heroes of our fiction. Impervious to the suffering around him, involved only in the mindless penance of survival, Sol is nevertheless haunted by hellish dreams of the camps—the only flaw in his perfect armor. The nightmares are the furies of his damnation, his only remaining contact with the terror of pain. In the eye of his dreams, the Pawnbroker experiences again with heightened clarity the degradation and death of his family, his own impotence and humiliation in trying to help them. The worst of his horrors, however, is what seems to him the unredeemable fact of his survival, brought back to him by the ghosts of his dream. Apparently nothing else is able to touch him. Yet underlying his cynical distrust of everything are remote tremors of his humanity. As he tells his assistant:

". . . I do not trust people and their talk, for they have created hell with that talk, for they have proved they do not deserve to exist for what they are."

"You too?" Ortiz asked, his voice faintly hoarse, as from too long a silence.

"I, too." [p. 87]

It is a judgment without exemptions, and it betrays for all the blackness of its vision an underlying moral (and human) commitment. Sol assumes responsibility, as human being, for the worst atrocities of behavior of his species—behavior which appears to him, by any stretch of possibility, unredeemable. The numbness which protects him from the horrors of the world serves also as his defense against himself—against the risk of trust.

If in the deadness of after-pain the Pawnbroker is beyond the pale of human feeling, he is not without human involvements. Out of his pawnshop earnings he supports his sister

Bertha's family in Mount Vernon in exchange for a place to live, and his mistress Tessie, a fellow-refugee from the camps, who lives with a kind of mourner's vigilance in the painful company of her dying father. Sol is himself committed for his livelihood to a racketeer named Albert Murillio, who uses the pawnshop as a front for the illegal profits of his other enterprises. Gradually, in their different ways, the Pawnbroker's involvements begin to impinge on him, to create pressures of nostalgia that violate the privacy of his indifference. The self-righteous badgering with which his sister and her husband persecute their withdrawn son Morton forces Sol into a begrudging sympathy for their victim and at the same time forces into recall the agony of his own persecution in the Nazi camps. Incidents of the present prefigure forgotten nightmares of the past. The cynical Murillio begins to seem to the Pawnbroker, through an accident of circumstance (Murillio owns a neighboring brothel —the Nazis had forced Sol's wife into a kind of prostitution), an agent of the same malevolence that destroyed his family— Sol himself an agent of that agent. Worse than that, Murillio, as numb to feeling in his own way as Sol, is a kind of alter ego to Sol's indifference—a monstrous paradigm of the implications of unfeeling. When Sol, burdened by the deepening pressures of guilt, tells Murillio of his need to end their partnership, the blandly vicious racketeer menaces him with a gun, threatens to kill him if he doesn't cooperate. The nightmare of the camps recalling itself in Murillio's brutality, Sol numbly acquiesces:

"I want only to be left in peace, to make the money I need and be left alone. I do not wish to lose the little I have, you understand, the store, the privacy. It was just that certain things have happened to me. . . ."
The sleek, carefully groomed head nodded understandingly. But the murderous eyes fixed on the Pawnbroker's mouth, growing a little bored even in menace. And that womanly attention to his mouth made it appear like some stare of twisted love to Sol, and he was terrified more than before. [p. 124]

Murillio's stare of acknowledgment provides a shock of recognition to Sol of the terrifying fact of his own complicity, an awareness of the corruption of feeling he shares in partnership with his persecutor. Moreover, in consenting to be Murillio's pawn, Sol has abetted, or so it seems to him, the very forces that have persecuted and deformed him. The burden of the awareness of his guilt, already impossibly heavy, continues to grow as he approaches the anniversary of his family's death. (Ritually, Sol must descend deeper into hell to recover the loss of himself before he can return to the world of the living.) In one of the most painful of his nightmares, he envisions, on the decapitated body of his child, the faces of all the physical and spiritual derelicts of his world "one after the other without end. . . ." They are all, he discovers, his unmourned children.

On the fifteenth anniversary of his family's death—the anniversary of his own spiritual death—Sol, pressured by his nightmares to the edge of breakdown, tremulously awaits the end: "He had been extinct for a long time, and only the carcass remained to be disposed of. Why, then, did he seize on the edge of the counter and tremble as he stared in terror at the sunlit doorway" (p. 183). The terror of the light is the terror of life. What more frightening to a man inexorably committed to the fact of his death! The Pawnbroker's anniversary day turns out, with somewhat intrusive allegorical contrivance, to be a waking nightmare of horrors—the final descent. One by one they arrive, the dancers of hell seeking redemption in the church of the pawnshop: a spastic lepidopterist, a jawless man, a cadaverous, decaying young woman, "a shuttering deviate," "a stone-faced, masculine-looking woman holding her pudgy Mongoloid son's hand," "an old, filthy pilgrim . . . like an apparition with a battered flashlight to pawn," "a blind, fat woman," a drug addict with the face of a jackal, and others, a seemingly endless stream of hellish deformities. And then, as a fit climax to this obscene parade, Murillio arrives to force Sol back into the partnership. With nothing to lose, his life of no value to him, Sol discovers himself invulnerable to the racketeer's threat. Unwilling to kill a man who wants to die, a man in some sense already dead ("I don't kick corpses"), Murillio relinquishes his claim and leaves the Pawnbroker to the freedom of his private torments. Sol's triumph over Murillio, however, is at the expense of certain painful losses of illusion—an awareness of uncharted fears.

The life-and-death confrontation with Murillio anticipates,

in the intensifying progression of horrors of Sol's day, the attempted robbery (and murder) to follow. Sol resists the robbers (Jesus' three partners in Halloween masks), provokes them with his resistance as he had Murillio, awaiting the mercy of death. When Robinson, the figure in the devil's mask (another alter ego to Sol's numbness) finally fires the gun at him, the shot hits and kills Jesus Ortiz, who has almost invisibly, at the last instant, stepped in the way. Jesus' death from the bullet meant for Sol is the ultimate consequence of their shared identity. In sacrificing himself for the Pawnbroker, he becomes Sol, he assumes the deepest identity of his teacher. If in his consciousness Jesus conceives the Pawnbroker's power and wisdom to come from money, in his dreams he envisions Sol as Christ: ". . . he glimpsed again, briefly, the figure of a heavy man awkwardly transfixed on a cross, a man with blue, cryptic numbers on his arm." (p. 182).

With Sol as his example, the assistant performs his own occasion of crucifixion, a means perhaps of possessing the Pawnbroker's mystery by enacting its implications. The fact of Jesus' sacrifice, an unlooked for miracle to Sol, brings the Pawnbroker back to sentient life. In the example of his assistant's humanity, Sol discovers the denied possibilities of his own. As Jesus moves out of life—a consequence of their shared communion—the Pawnbroker is resurrected. (By symbolic extension, Jesus' selfless nobility gives hope of renewal to an otherwise selfish and moribund world.) Overwhelmed by the sudden rush of life in him, Sol discovers after fifteen years of numbness the painful grace of tears, the joy of mourning. In crying for his assistant he is able at last to mourn for the death of his family, for all his losses, for all his dead. In discovering the shock of loss, he discovers the redemptive and agonizing wonder of love.

The achievement of the *The Pawnbroker* is in its rendering, in the luminous insights of its prose. The novel is always on the thin edge of going wrong, of letting its allegory control its direction, of teetering into bathos. Yet it survives. Wallant succeeds in making credible as experience, through the artifice of art, turns of events that would seem in the circumstance of raw material merely willful contrivance. In fact, much of the power of the novel resides in the tension of its risk. The prose is the transforming instrument. Sol's sudden comprehension of the meaning of Jesus' death, for example, accepts every risk of sentimentality and manages at once to be moving and true:

All his anesthetic numbness left him. He became terrified of the touch of air on the raw wounds. What was this great, agonizing sensitivity and what was it for? Good God, what was all this? *Love?* Could this be *love?* He began to laugh hysterically, and the voices in the store stopped. The mother cursed him from where she knelt over her dead son. [p. 200]

2

All of Wallant's novels have a similar, ritual structure: a man cut off from the source of himself, in a delicate truce with the nightmare of survival, slowly, terrifyingly, at the risk of everything, rediscovers the possibility of feeling. Whereas *The Human Season, The Pawnbroker,* and *The Children at the Gate,* are almost airlessly intense, *The Tenants of Moonbloom,* Wallant's next to last novel (actually, in fact, the last to be written), is an attempt at treating the same dark concerns, the same human dislocations, with something like comic perspective. Where the others are indebted in tenuous ways to the fiction of Malamud and Bellow (and Dostoevsky), *The Tenants of Moonbloom* is, in the only way the term is meaningful, an original achievement. And since it shows another aspect of the resources of Wallant's vision, I think it worth the attention of close analysis. *Moonbloom* is also the most beautifully written of the four novels, an uncannily funny and discomforting book.

As Sol Nazerman is a figure of tragedy, Norman Moonbloom is clearly a comic hero. Five feet seven inches high, a thirty-three year old virgin, a failed intellectual who collects rents from four decaying tenement buildings his brother owns (his brother's keeper), Moonbloom is only technically alive—"he traveled in an eggshell through which came only subdued light and muffled sound." Unlike the Pawnbroker, he has never suffered pain, only the vague sensitivity of its possibility. Where the Pawnbroker is spiritually dead, Moonbloom has never quite been born.

There had been no horrors in his life—only a slow widening of sensitivity. But he anticipated reaching the threshold of pain one of these days. It was like the fear of death; he could ignore it most of the time, although it was implacably there, to touch him with the very tip of its claw in moments of frustration, to bring dread to him during the 4:00 a.m. bladder call. The claw withdrew after just a touch, leaving him with a chronic, unrecognizable din that he did not think about; he was like a man who lives beside a foaming cataract and comes to take its roar for silence.[3]

The Tenants of Moonbloom is made up of a succession of comic and painful confrontations which work to push Norman across the "threshold of pain" into the exhilarating anguish of birth. The novel is about the awakening of Moonbloom and the quixotic implications of salvation. If it is Wallant's funniest book, it is also, as is the way with comic novels, his saddest and most pessimistic.

Wallant's unborn hero moves, as the ritual of habit demands, from the desolation of apartment to apartment, collecting rents and grievances with a dreamlike vagueness, a landlord's irritated indifference. With no life of his own, Norman, a passive recorder of the experience around him, unwittingly assumes some of the coloration of the lives of his tenants. At first indifferent to their needs, he gradually accepts their graces and deformities as a mirror of his own. After an extended illness, a long feverish sleep in which his life revisits him in a series of dreamlike recollections, Norman awakes as if resurrected, an imperceptibly new man. Having failed during fourteen years of college to find a calling in accounting, art, literature, dentistry, and the rabbinate, Norman discovers, in the vulnerability of after-illness, the wisdom of his deepest needs—the focus of purpose. Whereas before his illness he avoided the complication of involvement, afterwards he becomes, as a matter of chosen need, empathically involved in the frail destinies of his tenants.

The dreams of his life—his life itself dreamlike—have a kind of quintessential reality. In Wallant's rendering, the "flat pictures" of Norman's "hallucinatory reminiscence" become moments of illumination. As an example:

3 Edward Lewis Wallant, *The Tenants of Moonbloom* (New York: Harcourt, Brace & World, Inc., 1963), p. 8. All quotations are from this edition.

He is three and strawberry ice cream is New Year's Eve. His grandmother drops tears on him and holds him close. He licks the sweet pink cold. She wraps him in something light and soft and very strong. In the morning he will find it has become his skin. [p. 80]

As the blanket of skin (and the image of the eggshell earlier) suggests, Norman's muted life has been lived in a kind of placenta-like covering. By forcing him to confront the circumstances of his life, the fact of having been alive, his dreams violate the fragile shell of his protection and push him naked and tremulous into the world, in what appears to be, at least symbolically, a kind of second birth.

Weak as a newborn, he nevertheless realized that he had no way of avoiding whatever it was that had happened to him. Timidly he got up, and found that something had been torn away from him, that all the details of the room made deep impressions on his eyes. There was a blistering of plaster at the junction of wall and ceiling, the doorframe had a painted-over cut, the window shade was like worn skin, and he shuddered for it. He went into the bathroom and adjusted the water in the shower, solicitous of his frail, skinny body. The water drummed on him, wakening all his nerves. [pp. 81–82]

Norman re-enters the world with all his nerves exposed—a sensitized recorder of the wounds of his surroundings.

As the new Moonbloom goes his rounds, he finds himself suddenly involved, as a kind of spiritual arbiter, with the burdens and disguises of his tenants' lives. With the awakening of Norman's sensibility, the confrontations with the tenants become increasingly intimate and, in one way or another, he becomes a secret sharer of the griefs and disrepairs of each of them.

Unable to repair the breaks in the lives of his tenants, he decides—the next best alternative—to renovate their apartments, the blighted circumstances of their lives. Why does he elect to do it? The clownish candy butcher, Sugarman, a prophet to Norman's quixotic sainthood, defines the nature of his role for him, makes clear to Norman for the first time the undefined impulse of his responsibility.

"There is something masochistically inviting in the center of your racoon eyes. Like the little square of confection in *Alice in Wonder-*

land, there is written all over you 'Eat Me.' I know that with me I rant and rave in moving trains, deaf to my own voice and blind to the laughing faces. Only in here, in solitude, my voice rises to sound, and I wait for anyone to listen. And then you come along in your dark suit and vest and your pin in your lapel and your Al Capone hat, and you are like a queer microphone into which my pent-up words can pour. . . . Change your face, Moonbloom, or else listen and do something for us." [p. 139]

In Moonbloom's face, as Sugarman is quick to spot, is the revelation of his calling. He is an occasion for confession, a vessel for all the wounds and pains of spirit of his world, the cosmic victim as potential savior; yet salvation itself for his tenants seems beyond the pale of mortal sacrifice. All that remains as existential possibility for Moonbloom is the quixotic ritual of salvation—the repairing of defective objects, the disconnected extension of irreparable lives. The best he can do, within the limitations of mortality, is risk the impossible. In attempting to redeem the lives of his tenants, Norman discovers the extraordinary resources of his own nature. At the end, wild with exhilaration, Moonbloom becomes, the undiscovered country of his madness, himself.

Bruised and battered by his own seismographic apprehension of the wounds of his tenants, Norman becomes obsessive about repairing their long-neglected apartments as a means not so much of saving them but of surviving himself. Without funds to do the long list of things that need to be done—his brother is interested in profit not repair—Norman decides to make the renovations with his own hands (with the reluctant aid of the casually cynical Negro superintendent, Gaylord, one of the angels of Moonbloom's comic Christhood). Norman makes his decision after losing his virginity, at thirty-three, in a comic initiation to earth mother Sheryl Beeler, who lifts the scrawny rent collector over her and "immolates herself" with him. If Sheryl makes love to him merely for a cut in the rent, it is nevertheless an *act of love* for the rental agent—a belated baptism into manhood. A man (after all these years), Norman commits himself to the works of salvage and salvation, which seem to him the legacy of his manhood. At the same time he discovers, in a moment of luminous exhilaration, "that joy resembled mourning and was, if anything, just as powerful and profound." In an ecstasy of purpose, with the laughter of Lazarus, he begins the impossible chore of fixing "everything." When he informs Gaylord, Sancho Panza to his Quixote, of the "holy war" ahead of them, the superintendent can only moan. "Oh my God. . . . Oh my God almighty."

While renovating his tenants' apartments, Norman becomes more deeply than before a sharer of the agony of their lives. For example, while painting a charred wall in the Lublins' apartment he is witness to a terrible fight between Aaron Lublin and his blight of an uncle, who has moved in on Aaron's family uninvited, both refugees from the Nazi camps.

> And in the silence that followed, Norman knew that the old man would stay with them. For the Lublins, Hell was never over. But the constant pressure of Hell, its garish molten glow, was a sort of black light which threw their lives into strong relief and made them tangible, reassuring for each other. Unlike Norman, they had never doubted their existence. They knew their passions and their thresholds of pain. And, strangely, the persistent accompaniment of Hell's savage and wheedling voice also gave them whatever was the opposite of Hell. The fact was, they loved.
> Norman, covering the marks of the fire, caught the reflected light of their lives and changed color slightly himself. [p. 202]

If the worst of Norman's tenants burden him with the pain of their unfelt lives, the best of them, the Lublins, Paxton, Sugarman, Basellecci, are the sustenance of his spiritual growth. In his breakthrough, a version of breakdown, Norman's joy and anguish become inseparable. If sanity is unconcern, what other alternative for living in the world as a human being but madness!

The Tenants of Moonbloom moves uneasily across a delicate tight rope of risk between the comic and the pathetic. The last of Norman's renovations, the repair of Basellecci's swollen bathroom wall, serves to unify the two modes and to exemplify the profound, ambivalent sense of Norman's apparently senseless commitment. The obscenely swollen wall next to the toilet is a scatological joke in itself—the cause, so Basellecci has believed, of a terrible constipation. When Norman finally comes to repair the wall, its menace has ceased to concern Basellecci, who is dying of cancer: "the business of the wall . . . all a dream." To Norman, however, the wall remains as important as ever, the final purgation of his commitment to his tenants. In a comic nightmare scene, Gaylord, the "unfrocked plumber" Bodien, and Norman debate the problem of the swollen wall while getting drunk on Basellecci's liquor and the exaltation of their collaborative madness, while the mournful Basellecci looks on, dying, coming to life in the communion of their excitement.

None of Norman's repairs have any significant effect on the griefs of his tenants. Yet the terror of this knowledge only intensifies him in his purpose. His commitment exists purely for itself, without influence of gain. That his renovations are gratuitous endows them with a kind of special grace, an innocence of purpose. Norman's works of salvage are performed not for his tenants but for himself (the tenants have "entered him"), out of the deepest demands of his own need.

When Norman attacks the wall with a pickax, he becomes inundated by a "brown thick liquid," purging the building of all its corruption. As the tenants have "entered him" so has he assumed the corruptions of their lives. Norman declaims in his frenzy, a spokesman for them all, "I'M BORN." The joke of Norman covered with shit, announcing his birth, is cosmic and seems in context—Norman surrounded admiringly by his three drunken disciples—a revelation, a kind of miracle. When he leaves, transfigured by the experience, the snow has melted and, as if in universal acknowledgment of his potency, the scent of spring is in the air. In his quixotic way, Norman has, it seems, saved us all.

The achievement of Wallant's four novels resides mostly, I think, in their revelation of character, in their ability to make sense of the dark extremes of human behavior we share in communal possibility, the best and worst of us. Out of the final depths of depravity and horror, Wallant's children of darkness discover the terrible luxury of feeling that provides, at the price of pain, the redemptive possibility of love.

10 · Wake Before Bomb:

Ceremony in Lone Tree by Wright Morris

> For more than a century the territory ahead
> has been the world that lies somewhere be-
> hind us, a world that has become, in the last
> few decades, a nostalgic myth.
> —*The Territory Ahead*

WRIGHT MORRIS was born in Nebraska in 1910. He has the distinction among serious contemporary writers of being neither
southerner nor Jew nor Negro nor Catholic nor expatriate; and
if that alone weren't enough to disqualify him from being a
talented American novelist, he is over fifty and apparently at
the height of his powers. A holdover from another generation,
a late rose from an earlier summer, he is a Midwesterner writing
about the vanished trail, chronicling the moral erosion of our
sterile and sterilizing civilization. Unlike many of his fellows,
prodigious infants whose first words are so phenomenal they are
unable to learn new ones, Morris' twelfth novel, *Ceremony in
Lone Tree* (1960), is by and large his best, incomparably better
than his first. Without pandering to popular taste, without
mimicking himself, Morris has continually improved, defining
and intensifying his vision. This is as it should be and so rarely
is in this depleting climate of ours, in which talents are often
dried up before they have ripened to maturity.

Morris' novels are written as if perceived by a slow-motion
camera. In all but *The Huge Season, Love among the Cannibals,* and *What a Way To Go,* almost nothing happens, but
what does is lingered over, seen in photographic close-up, illuminating the patterned grain of experience. The rhythms of his
writing are deliberate, inhibited, drugged, at times hardly perceptible, evoking the slow pulse beat of the atrophied life he
renders. Ironically, his world is most active in still life. For
example, *Ceremony in Lone Tree* opens:

Come to the window. The one at the rear of the Lone Tree Hotel.
The view is to the west. There is no obstruction but the sky. Although there is no one outside to look in the yellow blind is drawn
low at the window, and between it and the pane a fly is trapped.
He has stopped buzzing. Only the crawling shadow can be seen.
Before the whistle of the train is heard the loose pane rattles like a
simmering pot, then stops, as if pressed by a hand, as the train
goes past. The blind sucks inward and the dangling cord drags in the
dust on the sill.[1]

Yet underlying the flickering stillness of his world is the
primordial violence and horror which shakes it, which gives it
what little movement it has. With the exception of *The Field
of Vision*, which won the National Book Award of 1957, none
of Morris' novels explicitly investigates (as do the novels of
most of his serious contemporaries) the burden of guilt imposed
by participation in a self-destroying world. Insofar as any of
Morris' heroes—or, more exactly, antiheroes—is made aware of
the chaos in which he participates, he is vaguely disturbed by
what he senses is his own inadequacy. Yet Morris' characters,
like Hemingway's fabled icebergs, are seven-eighths submerged
and are rarely conscious of the causes of their dissatisfaction,
are conscious only that they are dissatisfied. Where there is
a sort of personal salvation through racking experience in the
works of such writers as Bellow, Malamud, Wallant, and
Flannery O'Connor, Morris' sufferers, victims of an arbitrarily
malevolent universe, are, with rare exception, never permitted the grace of redemption. Instead, Morris often
employs a conscience character, less an authorial spokesman than an authorial sensibility, a rarefied seismograph,
who picks up in magnification the unexpressed tremors
of his race. Webb in *The Deep Sleep* is one, so is the
Boy in *Man and Boy*, Lawrence in *The Huge Season*,
and Boyd in both *The Field of Vision* and *Ceremony in Lone
Tree*. A variant is the unwitting sacrifice, the redeemer in spite
of himself: Will Brady, the man who thought he was Santa
Claus, in *The Works of Love*; Paula Kahler, the man who
relinquished his manhood, in *The Field of Vision*; Lawrence,

---

1 Wright Morris, *Ceremony in Lone Tree* (New York: Atheneum,
1960), p. 1. All quotations are from this edition.

the parody of Gatsby, in *The Huge Season*; Lee Roy Momeyer, the adolescent killer who was "tired of being pushed around," in *Ceremony in Lone Tree*. What Faulkner has created for Mississippi, Morris seems to be attempting for Nebraska—the founding of a self-contained mythic world in which the universe can be dissected and examined in miniature.

Where earlier western writers dealt with the winning of the land, Morris deals with the losing of it—the physical and moral ravage of the land by civilization. The main preoccupations of Morris' novels: prohibitive isolation, violence repressed and exploded, the castrating female, the castrated male, the unlived life, the narcosis of nostalgia, the "self-unmade man," the whimsical nature of the universe, are all assembled as if for the occasion in *Ceremony in Lone Tree*. The nominal occasion is Scanlon's ninetieth birthday, for which an odd collection of relatives, friends, and strangers come together, instinctively searching for their own identity—their very existence—in the collective identity of the group. For each, in one way or another, the ceremony is an attempt to discover the source of his life by recapturing his vanished, often hallucinatory, past. Scanlon, like Hightower in Faulkner's *Light in August*, has over the years kept the past intact by seeing nothing but the reflection of his own internal reality. The mythic past serves as a preservative, enabling Scanlon, the man who knew Buffalo Bill, who had come to believe he *was* Buffalo Bill, to go on existing long after the real life in him had snapped. All that is left in Lone Tree, the last outpost of the old West—the rest has been dessicated by "progress"—is the deserted hotel where Scanlon lives, the one fruitless tree that gives the place its name, as tough and fragile as the old man himself, and Scanlon's private view of the town, the same view he has held unwaveringly, though the town has withered away, for some forty years. Morris evokes Scanlon's internally imposed reality—objectifies it—permitting us, as initiates into the mysteries, to enter the experience of his unique vision:

Nothing irked him [Scanlon] more than to hear from his children that the place was empty, the town deserted, and that there was nothing to see. He saw plenty. No matter where he looked. Down the tracks to the east, like a headless bird, the bloody neck still raw and dripping, a tub-shaped water tank sits high on stilts. Scanlon once saw a coon crawl out the chute and drink from the spout. Bunches of long-stemmed grass, in this short-grass country, grow where the water drips between the rails, and Scanlon will tell you he has seen a buffalo crop it up. A big bull, of course, high in the shoulders, his short tail like the knot in a whip, walking on the ties like a woman with her skirts tucked up. Another time a wolf, half crazed by the drought, licked the moisture from the rails like ice and chewed on the grass like a dog out of sorts. On occasion stray geese circled the tank like a water hole. All common sights, according to Scanlon, where other men squinted and saw nothing but the waves of heat, as if the cinders of the railbed were still on fire. [p. 5]

The old man is unable to live in the split-level, glass-walled houses of his grandchildren because they permit him no view of his reality. If Scanlon has no present, that is, retains the past as the present, for the most part the others have neither present nor past, have discarded the past and its traditions without having a real present to take its place. In place of the traditions of the frontier, they have retained, like relics amid their antiseptic houses and supercharged cars, illusory memories of the "good-old bygone days." Nostalgia is their anesthetic against the pain of living. For the sleepwalkers, the surface of life is quiescent, but the violence underlying it, suppressed by euphemism, erupts at the slightest provocation, waking them momentarily into the nightmare of the real world. As quickly as they are awakened, however, they drift off again into the "couldn't be happier" dream which sustains them, permits them to go on affirming their nonlife as life in spite of everything.

Though Morris is unsympathetic to the sterile and bloodless existence of the Scanlon clan, he is not unsympathetic to the people themselves. They are victims, possessed from within by the flabby devils of a machine-devitalized civilization and haunted from without by a malevolent universe. Though bemused by their self-parody, Morris is compassionate toward their plight, toward the unresolved and unresolvable ambiguities of their existence. In an unreal world bent on destroying itself, is it better, the novel asks, to be awake to the nightmare—a live sufferer—or to sleep, comforted by dreams of an earlier and nobler age? Boyd, the conscience of Morris' world, a man who has even failed at failure, is aware of the dilemma, though no less helpless for his self-knowledge. He makes the pilgrimage from Acapulco to Lone Tree for no apparent reason, just as McKee, who both fears and admires Boyd, has on blind impulse invited him, an outsider, to a family reunion. Both are motivated by nostalgia, the romantic hope that by coming together, as ever boyhood chums (both are now past sixty), they can recapture the past and with it their youthful possibilities. The dream persists for both despite their mutually disturbing encounter the previous year in Mexico (*The Field of Vision*).

Boyd and McKee, and the "only woman on God's green earth" for both of them, McKee's wife, née Lois Scanlon, make up the center of interest of the novel, if it can be said to have a fixed center. (Scanlon, the Lone Tree, is the abiding symbol and focal point). Boyd is the artist, the clown, the defective saint and hero—a man who tried to walk on water and failed; McKee is the spectator, the nonparticipant, a man in need of a hero, for whom Boyd performs. They are Quixote and Sancho. While Boyd, retaining the nostalgic illusion of boyhood, continues to behave like a boy (squirting soda pop in the face of a bull at a Mexican *corrida*), McKee continues to do nothing except watch Boyd and marvel at him. His function is symbolized in pressing the electronic button that opens his garage doors. Lois, the frigid "dream-girl" ("if she could have one wish in the world it would be to live where there were no guns, nor anything you could point at anyone"), having to choose between the two, has taken the vicarious boy rather than risk the potential threat of the real one. Lois, awakened to life for the first and only time by Boyd, has chosen McKee and security, McKee and dominance, McKee and inviolability, McKee and sleep. Despite her rejection of potency, she is fascinated by guns, that is deathly afraid of them, and as a precaution against the possibility of his manhood, all but devours her grandchild Gordon, named like her son after the rejected saint Gordon Boyd. Lois, like Mother in *Man and Boy*, Mrs. Porter in *The Deep Sleep*, Billie Harcum in *Love among the Cannibals*, is one of Morris' archetypal American women—the castrating female. Though aware of what she is, Boyd has dedicated himself to what she represents, the American dream goddess—the hero's reward.

The trip to Lone Tree is for Boyd, as for the others, a pilgrimage to his past. En route, he is confronted by the present. When he stops at a hotel in Nevada, a kind of decadent Mecca in Morris' cosmos, Boyd is asked if he wants to be awakened for the bomb:

For the bomb? He saw that it was a routine question.
Just before dawn, she replied. That was when the breeze died, and they did it. When he didn't reply she said if he hadn't seen a bomb go off, he should. He owed it to himself. Terrible as it was, it was also a wonderful sight. There was this flash, then the pillar of fire went up and up, like a rabbit's ear.
Boyd turned as if he saw it.
"You'd better be up for it," she said, and after his name in the register she added: WAKE BEFORE BOMB. [pp. 30–31]

Despite its nightmare implications, this is a comic scene; yet as the image of the bomb continues to loom, it becomes increasingly horrifying.

"Mr. Boyd," said the woman, "there was no bomb, so I didn't wake you up."
"Maybe next time," he said.
"Oh, there'll be a next time all right," she replied. "Maybe tonight. Where'll you be tonight?" [p. 39]

The landlady's guarantee haunts Boyd as the threat of the bomb haunts the world of the novel. Next time? When?

The bomb, which significantly never goes off in the novel (at least not as bomb) is the present without a future which haunts the past, a reality haunting a dream. Morris employs the image of the bomb, "a pillar of fire going up and up like a rabbit's ear," as a source for the various explosions of violence which shake the quiescent scene. Any startling sound (the backfire of a car, the explosion of a train passing nearby at high speed, the report of an old pistol) or flash of light (the flickering of a neon sign, the newly risen sun illuminating the plain as if from within, the setting sun spreading like a forest fire somewhere off in the near distance) and Boyd—or Mrs. Boyd, his newly acquired traveling companion—wonders if the bomb has finally gone off. Disparate lights and shapes are transformed in his mind into the same nightmare image—"the pillar of fire."

Wake before bomb is contemporary civilization's equivalent of the old religious exhortation, repent before it is too late! Morris ironically wonders whether it is worth it in either case. Though the Nebraska residents in their deep sleep are not aware that they expect the bomb—though they do expect something—Boyd as their conscience expects it for them. The bomb is their judgment, and Boyd wonders whether waking them for it will do any conceivable good. He reasons:

"To wake before the bomb was to risk losing all to gain what might be so little—a brief moment in the present, that one moment later joined in the past. Nevertheless, as the lady said, it was a wonderful sight. . . . To wake before the bomb was tricky business. What if it scared you to sleep?" [p. 32]

In the end, it scares Boyd to sleep. His generalized conjecture becomes a personally fulfilled prophecy.

On another level, it scares Scanlon to sleep too. The explosion of a gunshot (which Boyd associates with the bomb) startles Scanlon from a deathlike sleep, wakens him from the past to confront him with the present. The confrontation kills him, in a sense scares him to death. Jennings, the son of Will Brady (the protagonist of Works of Love and a contemporary of Scanlon's), accosts Scanlon with his identity:

Raising on his elbow, Jennings peered through the moonlight and said, "That you, Scanlon?" just as the old man dropped as if through a hole in the floor. Hardly a sound, no more noise than if a suit of clothes had slipped off a hanger, and the man who had worn them had vanished into thin air. [p. 277]

His death is a kind of extinction; the present, like an apocalyptic bomb, wiping out all traces of the past. Morris gives the death all the aspects of a religious miracle. Scanlon, as if transported, or perhaps disintegrated, vanishes "into thin air." Jennings, his symbolic son, by identifying him, forces Scanlon into a confrontation with his present self—his dead self—which kills him. In fact, when, after hearing the shot, McKee discovers Jennings leaning over Scanlon's body, he suspects that Jennings has actually shot him.

Scanlon's daughter Lois would have it that her father died in his sleep. By euphemizing his death she denies her father his last small moment of heroism—his facing of himself. Her life's sleep disturbed by the threat of male potency, Lois feels compelled to castrate all men in order to keep herself inviolate, in order to get her beauty rest. A recurrent concern in Morris' novels is the continuous war between male and female, in which woman, the more instinctively predatory, usually emerges victorious.

The gratuitous eruptions of violence which shatter the Nebraska stillness are, Morris suggests, misdirected assertions of male potency in a society dominated, smothered, and emasculated by the female. Lee Roy Momeyer's running over of two classmates who have taunted him and Charlie Munger's twelve sniper murders are, as analogues to the bomb, explosions of repressed sexual energy—the violence of impotence. The sign in front of the gas station at which Lee Roy worked suggests the correspondence: HAVE GUNS—WILL LUBRICATE. A sport of nature, inordinately puny, Lee Roy is as murderer a victim and sacrifice to the latent violence of his contemporaries; he permits them to satisfy their own unexpressed blood lusts vicariously. Humiliated by his "biggers," including his "dream goddess" cousin Etoile, who bears an amazing resemblance to her Aunt Lois (the present mimicking the past), Lee Roy finally and insistently demonstrates that he does indeed have guns. As he explains it, "I guess I just got tired of being pushed around." The boys he mowed down with his '37 Ford hot rod were dressed in women's clothes, mocking Lee Roy's apparent lack of masculinity. In return, he performs the male role, impregnating the women-dressed-men with death.

After Christmas he drove back to school and everything was all right, nothing happened all morning. His car started all right when it was time to leave. But when he headed down the driveway he could see them, Bobo Lamkin wearing a girl's gym bloomers, the other two with old ladies' hats on their heads. When Lee Roy gave a toot on his his horn, they all looked at the sky. Where the walks had been shoveled, half the student body waited to see what Lee Roy would do, and he could see their faces in the laboratory windows on the second floor. He saw Etoile, taller than Mrs. Ansley, on the steps of the library, wearing the rubber boots that gave her

blisters on both feet. "F—k the bastards," Lee Roy said, gripped
the wheel like he did the oilcan and heard the gas hiss in the car-
buretors as he gave it the gun. Allowing for the fact that the drive
was slippery, it did pretty well. Two of them didn't budge, but Stu
Smiley, hearing his kid sister scream at him, got one leg into the
snowdrift, and the fender caught him just right to spin him around.
Lee Roy felt the weight of the other two as if he had thumped
into a snowbank, and Bobo Lamkin stayed on the hood till Lee Roy
came to a stop. In his rearview mirror the kids standing on the steps
looked the way they did in the class picture, not one of them
moving, only one of them making a sound. Stu Smiley lay with his
head pushed in the snowbank, whimpering like a dog. [p. 126]

By having Lee Roy the nephew of Lois' sister, Morris gives the
epidemic of isolated acts of violence immediate reference to the
central action of the novel; in effect, he gives the latent menace
of the bomb a personal correlative. Maxine expresses in sim-
plistic terms Morris' explanation for the contagion of these
oddly gratuitous crimes. " 'I swear to God it's the bomb or
something, everybody's crazy' " (p. 116). Whether it is a symp-
tom or a cause of the mass insanity, the bomb is, Morris insists,
at least a factor.

Everybody *is* to some extent "crazy" in Morris' novel. In the
same area, at about the time Lee Roy runs down his persecutors,
another young boy has been shooting down, with a kind of
arbitrary fairness, complete strangers, terrorizing the community. After he has killed an even dozen (the resultant hysteria
is responsible for several other injuries), he is caught and
identified as Charlie Munger, a local boy, "who," as he tells
the police, "wanted to be somebody." The violence is an asser-
tion of identity, of being, the agonized death throes of life on
the verge of extinction. A contemporary of Lee Roy and Munger,
Etoile, a representative of the present, understands and empha-
thizes with their impulses. About Lee Roy: " 'He ran over two
bullies, and I don't blame him' " (p. 116). About Charlie
Munger:

"You want to know why?" she yelled. "It's because nobody wants
to know why. It's because nobody want to know *any-thing*! Everybody hates everybody, but nobody knows why anybody gets shot.
You want to know somethin'? I'd like to shoot a few dozen people
myself!" [p. 117]

So would many another of Morris' ordinary, respectable people.
As the "civilization" of the present destroys the traditions of the
past, the younger generation, their normal energies inhibited,
explode into violence against their elders, destroying the remnants of the past in their opposition to the present. Like D. H.
Lawrence, to whom he is somewhat indebted, Morris points out
that the smoother, that is the more euphemistic and sterile the
surface of life becomes, the more the primordial forces erupt
into meaningless violence.

Those of the middle generation, like McKee, who have ex-
changed "living" for the comfort of unconsciousness (McKee
"couldn't be happier"), have retreated into a kind of somnam-
bulism; they are suddenly shaken into uneasy wakefulness by
the unaccountable violence of their unrecognizable progenies.
This is symbolized for us by McKee's unsuccessful attempt at
drowning a wounded bird:

> When the small body had resisted drowning, he had lost his
> nerve. He had thought it lifeless, but when its life was threatened,
> it had stiffened like a steel spring, hissed like a dragon and looked
> at him with such hate he had dropped it in the weeds and run for
> his life. Where did it get such courage? Could it be found in the
> small battered head or that tiny heart? Had McKee, in threatening
> a bird, threatened life itself? [p. 51]

The act of running from the pulsing life of the broken bird is
intended to define McKee's role, but, in addition, it symbolizes
the threat that life, personified by the young, imposes on those
who would deny its existence. Awakened momentarily, confronted by the horror of the present, he is frightened back to
sleep—frightened into the illusory past.

The purpose of the reunion is not so much to celebrate
Scanlon's birthday (the past) but to plan the elopement of Etoile
and Calvin (the future). Calvin, who looks like Gary Cooper,
is a throwback to the old West where men rode horses, shot
guns, and lived "without externally imposed discipline." His
world denied him by "progress," Calvin has developed a stutter,
a manifestation of unreconciled rebellion, which to all intents
and purposes makes him mute. Etoile and Eileen are both aware
of Calvin's potential violence and are anxious to domesticate
him before he does himself or someone else some harm. Pro-

voked by the sex-conscious Etoile into raping her (all their acts
of love are performed like death struggles), Calvin performs
the sex act as compulsively, as violently as Lee Roy commits
murder.

Calvin runs away to retain his freedom, to rediscover the
vanished West, the world his grandfather Scanlon has described
to him. Panning for gold with an old prospector, Calvin senses
that he has found his grandfather's Eden. However, even in the
monastic hills of the "past," he is confronted by the "civilized"
present—a uranium prospector with a geiger counter. The in-
truder in his strange outfit appears as a kind of Martian invader
to Calvin, a violator of his grandfather's land. Like the old timer
Mr. Fischer, Calvin is embittered by the confrontation:

> Without having seen the face of this man he hated him. If he
> had his gun along he might have taken a few pot shots at him.
> This was his grandfather's country, Mr. Fischer's country, and it
> was now Calvin McKee's country, to be defended from these cheat-
> ers the way you'd scare off cattle thieves. [p. 98]

Calvin, his "life threatened by the machine, is roused to murderous anger. A defender of the past he is enraged to see the
land violated by civilization. Not unlike Lee Roy, Calvin does
not want to be pushed around, but his rage is never given occasion to erupt. As he is returning home from the hills, Calvin
is picked up as a suspect for the sniper murders. From his stutter
and weather-beaten appearance, he seems to the police, as he
does to his own mother, a likely possibility. Having secured his
release from jail, his mother ironically admonishes him: " 'My
darling,' she said, putting her finger to his lips, 'don't shoot a
dozen people unless they're policemen.' She kissed him, then
added, 'It's not worth the trouble, sweetheart. It's been done' "
(p. 106). It has been done, in a sense, for Calvin. Munger has
unwittingly been the agency for Calvin's unexpressed rage—his
spokesman, as it were.

The rages of the middle generation are for the most part
repressed (although Lois cannot resist firing one of Scanlon's
guns, aiming at nothing but the oppressive world in general).
These rages shake the surface ever so slightly like Morris' image
of the no longer buzzing fly trapped between the window and
the blind. When her small grandson Gordon, whose constant

play at guns imposes a latent threat to his elders, announces that he doesn't want to play with girls, Lois' reaction is unwarrantedly violent. "For all her love and need of him she could have put his head into a bowl and held it under" (p. 160). She is afraid of the physical life in Gordon in much the same way that McKee felt threatened by the wounded bird. As Gordon violently resists Lois' attempts to mute his masculinity, she in turn violently resists his assertions of maleness. The violence proliferates itself like the chain reaction of the bomb. When Gordon points one of Scanlon's guns at the usually docile Maxine, she slaps him sharply across the face and bellows at him as if he had, in fact, attacked her:

"I will not stand for that, you hear?"
Jennings doubted that the boy did. He tried with all his might to pull the trigger. "Bang!" he screamed. "You're dead!" With her other hand Maxine slapped him hard across the mouth. He sucked in his lip as if to see if he still had it, then set his mouth in a line that made him look years older. Jennings recognized the face as that of Mrs. McKee. [p. 188]

Had Jennings not a moment before taken the bullets from the gun, Gordon could conceivably have killed Maxine. The enraged Gordon's resemblance to Mrs. McKee anticipates her insane firing of the same gun later in the novel.

Even ordinarily gentle people like Bud Momeyer, Lee Roy's uncle, have violent atavistic preoccupations. That Bud (his name suggests his generalized identity) experiences life vicariously through the lives of the various people on his mail route suggests that Morris intends him as a kind of cipher—a passive recorder of universal experience. For this reason, Bud's propensity for killing harmless animals can be seen as a manifestation or transference of the repressed violence he senses about him. Bud, who has been working on a self-filling fountain pen, gives up inventing when he inherits from a taxidermist an antique bow and a set of feathered arrows over twenty years old. Bud rejects the artificial concerns of the present for the primal experiences of the past—but it is a past distorted by the uncongenial demands made on it by the present. Not quick enough to shoot wild rabbits with his bow and arrows, Bud, out of an instinctive need for self-realization, becomes an impassive hunter of alley cats. Intending only to frighten the animal, or so he believes, Bud kills his first cat:

> The weight of the arrow turned the tom half way around. Bud could see the arrow on one side of him and the feathers on the other, just before he stepped off the roof and dropped to the ground.
> Not a sound. Not a whimper. Nor was it in any way messy. Bud did not feel bad. He did not feel much of anything. [pp. 114–15]

Bud reacts as if there were no direct correspondence between the pulling of the bow and the death of the cat. Yet he goes on killing cats out of blind compulsion, avoiding the moral consequences of the act by divorcing the intention from the deed. He experiences a benumbed elation at his "mystic" potency, as if he had killed by merely pointing his finger at the doomed object. Bud is a spiritual child, amoral rather than immoral, an innocent killer, an inadvertent agent of his society. Unable to restrain the least of his compulsions, Bud hunts and kills the Ewing's prize bulldog whom they have pampered as if he were the child of their loins. The discovery of the arrow-pierced carcass is a piece of nightmare comedy in the best tradition of Faulkner's *As I Lay Dying*.

In ironic juxtaposition, the grief-stricken Ewings (Mrs. Ewing is one of Scanlon's daughters) drive off in their Cadillac-pulled trailer to deliver the body of their dog to the insurance company, while at the same time, McKee, in a mule-driven cart, drives the uninsured, unmourned Scanlon to burial. The two funeral processions are comments on one another. In the world of the sterile present, the show dog is more highly valued than the man. It is no wonder a man is impelled to commit murder to assert himself.

Boyd and Mrs. Boyd provide between them a kind of Greek chorus on the action of the novel. Of the two, only Boyd is even peripherally a participant in the action. As I mentioned before, Boyd is the novel's conscience. Disillusioned by the world into a pose of uncommitment, he has courted failure out of guilt, out of a personal commitment to the larger failure of the civilization as a whole. He does not scavenge his society, he heckles it. The uncommitted Mrs. Boyd—Boyd is mistaken in thinking he too is uncommitted—is an inadvertent Cassandra, an ingenuous and phophetic commentator on the static scene. Mrs. Boyd, who attaches herself to Boyd because he is very like the husband she has just divorced, has a basic response (with small variation) to whatever she finds incredible—"Sweet Jesus!"—and she finds almost everything incredible. It is at once a curse and a prayer, so apt that it becomes infectious. Etoile, Eileen, Maxine, and little Gordon all mimic her imprecation, as if it somehow explained life or at least placated it. When she first meets Boyd in a Nevada bar, she sees through his clown façade, as if he were, like McKee's new house, three sides glass:

"You know what? You probably sounded just like him [her husband]. The friggin good old days. . . ."
"I got news for you," she said. "You're just like him. The friggin brainy type. . . . You think we meet the same people over and over? He's so friggin scared of everything, like you are. . . . If you're like Irwin you met the only real friggin woman of your life back in High School. That's all, you just met her. Lucky for you she married somebody else." [pp. 35–36]

She is an inveterate truth-teller and Boyd brings her along to the ceremony as a kind of self-protecting stunt, to give himself courage and to bring the others truth. She has achieved the failure that Boyd has lacked the courage to pursue into its final Hell. This explains her purity and her second sight, and his imperfect vision for all his intelligence and sensibility. When in the middle of his journey, Boyd is forced to abandon his car (an old Plymouth from the "good old days") in a ditch and board a train, he discovers that he has left the engine running. It is an act definitive of his life as a whole. He is unable to break with the past, but continues to invest live energy into its dead memory, a victim of his own nostalgia. As he rides up front with the brakeman, he has a momentary insight:

He gripped the rail, his eyes on the tracks that drew the two halves of the plain together, like a zipper, joining at the rear what it had just divided at the front. Why, he wondered, reaching toward the girl, did things coming toward him seem to break into pieces, and things that receded into the past seem to make sense? [p. 46]

The present is frightening because its meanings are fragmentary and uncertain, the past comforting because its truths are static (though adjustable) and secure. Morris' comment about Scott Fitzgerald in *The Territory Ahead*, that "he was the first of his generation to know that life is *absurd*," tells us as much about Morris as about Fitzgerald. Boyd knows, or thinks, that "life is absurd," and thus it is impossible for him to take the present seriously. In order to continue to exist, he escapes into his home-made illusions of the past—into ironic self-pity.

When the girl asks him why he wants her along, he tells her: " 'They take me for a clown. We're going to clown it up' " (p. 42). At the ceremony in Lone Tree, Boyd is as good as his word. His clowning, however, like that of Shakespeare's fools, becomes a means of telling the truth in ironic guise. At first Boyd sits quietly, a spectator rather than a participant, withdrawn into his recollections of the past, until Lois, aroused by memory, taunts him by calling him a clown. Boyd responds to the stimulus:

"Daughter, [Boyd and Mrs. Boyd address each other as "daughter" and "daddy"] it's later than you think. I'm clowning it up before the bomb."
"Bomb?" said Edna [Mrs. Ewing]. "What bomb?"
"The *bomb*, Sweet Jesus. He's got this friggin bomb on the brain. He won't be happy till it goes off—will you, Daddy?"
"Let there be light, Daughter. The Lord said, 'Let there be light.' " [p. 172]

Light symbolizes judgment as well as dawn as well as truth. It is is a grim joke, meant in earnest, and it is only the beginning of Boyd's "clowning it up." Aroused to his "fool's" obligations, he has a sense of mission as conscience and Doomsday prophet to bring truth to the citizens of Lone Tree—to wake them before the bomb. In shaking them from their slumber, Boyd becomes, as catalyst, their personalized bomb.

At the dinner table, Boyd's messianic clowning becomes more explicitly personal. He chides McKee for being afraid to show his feelings—for euphemizing his life out of existence.

"Boyd," said McKee, "I hope you didn't come back just to stir up old feelings."
"Or is it new ones, McKee? Not the past but the present. In the good old days we both had feelings. How is it now? On good

authority I have it that you and Mrs. McKee couldn't be happier. What scares you pissless is not the fear of death, but the fear of exposure. The open fly of your feelings. You know why? You might not have any. What can one do? Keep the upper lip firmly pleated. I see that Mrs. McKee is wearing one now, like a veteran's poppy. How well it becomes her." [p. 181]

It is a virulent diatribe directed not only at McKee and Lois but at all of them, including himself. Boyd is not content to let things be, but out of the same messianic impulse that led him as a boy to try to walk on water, he is bent on curing his society by lancing its evils. Ultimately, he fails at cleansing the world, just as he failed to walk on water. Like Gatsby, he is unable to live up to his incredibly romantic ideal of himself. He is, after all, a defunct hero, in a world in which heroism has gone out of fashion. In his own way, he is as obsolescent as Scanlon. For all his efforts, he is doomed to remain an unredeemer, himself guilt-ridden and unredeemed.

The end of the novel is like the ending of Pope's *Dunciad*, in which dullness and chaos reign over all. McKee, the apotheosis of dullness, rhapsodizes wishfully about a future as fruitful as the vanished past, while Boyd (and Mrs. Boyd) the safeguarders of wakefulness, sleep. "Aloud McKee said, 'It's going to be a hot one,' and turned to see why they paid him no heed. The old man was past caring. The two on the car seat were asleep" (p. 304). In attempting to wake McKee, Boyd succeeds only in falling asleep himself, leaving the unreal world to the province of the unreal.

Before the final capitulation of the life of the past, symbolized by Scanlon's death, Boyd resurrects it for a time, inciting the Scanlon clan to small moments of self-discovery and truth-saying. At Scanlon's death the rebellion dies, and the family is once more anesthetized. Out of sentimental response they unite in concern around the corpse of a man who had ceased to concern them at all while he lived. The appeal of death in Morris' grass-less world is stronger than the appeal of life. Boyd responds ironically to the McKees' sentimental reverence of death—a kind of implicit necrophilia. Parodying Lois' "he died in his sleep," Boyd quips what she really meant: " 'It died while we slept' " (p. 284).

If Boyd is the conscience of his society, its most exceptional member, McKee is its most unexceptional representative. Strangely enough, though one would hardly notice it without making count, McKee is the focal consciousness of one more chapter than is Boyd. This is not to say that McKee is the protagonist; Boyd is the more interesting and more sympathetic character. Yet Boyd's iconoclastic intelligence is on the outside looking in, while McKee is in himself a manifestation of the very unreality to which Boyd objects. While Boyd is our spiritual guide into Morris' haunted world, McKee is the world —the essential incorporeality at which Boyd points our attention. McKee's vision is from the inside of things. His half-comprehended discovery of the inescapable reality of evil is even more an illumination of Morris' world view than is Boyd's vituperative insight. Harassed by a group of youths, McKee has an immediate if terrifying revelation:

> As men come and go, he was not easily frightened—in case he was, he could make a show of nerve—but the grinning faces of those young hoodlums scared him worse than he dared to admit. McKee had recognized the nameless face of evil—he recognized it, that is, as stronger than the nameless face of Good. Everybody talked about Good, but had McKee ever set eyes on it? Had he ever felt pure Good? No, but he had come face to face with evil. He had seen the underside of the rock. What troubled him was not what he saw, but the nameless appetite behind it, the lust for evil in the faces of the beardless boys. McKee felt more life in their life than in himself. He didn't want a showdown. He felt himself beaten at the start. If McKee represented Good, like the Gray Ladies on the war posters, then the forces of Evil would carry the day. [p. 51]

What McKee avoids recognizing is that he, his generation, has spawned these "evil youths"; he has, in a sense, denied them into existence. Though immediately afterward McKee shuts out the implications of his awareness, taking refuge in the nostalgic past, his terrible vision (Morris' vision) remains, haunting the world of the novel. Good is the veneer under which evil resides in Morris' imbalanced Manichean universe. Unaccountable eruptions of evil, explosions of repressed energy, vitalize the otherwise static surface. It is Charlie Munger and not McKee who shakes his world. Evil in *Ceremony* is invested with primordial life, while good manifests itself in a disbelief in evil, in a refusal to recognize even the possibility of its existence. Consequently, in Morris' dessicated Plains, evil is potent, good, impotent.

If there is no redemption in the world of *Ceremony in Lone Tree*, there is guilt and terror and suffering—the tremors of redemption quested and unachieved. Less obviously talented than the most exciting of his contemporaries, Morris has in many ways, through the concentration of his craft and his ability to define and articulate the comic despair of his nihilistic vision, outperformed them—if not with any single book, with the bulk of his achievement. He has had the courage to say no in a civilization whose euphemistic yea-saying in the face of potential annihilation has been indicative in itself of the profound reaches of its self-denial. Yet this very courage is the source not only of the strength of Morris' vision, I suspect, but of its final limitation. He lacks the over-riding compassion which enables Bellow, for example, to redeem his lost sufferers in the midst of impossible circumstances. Morris' world, in which the past and future merge in malevolent conspiracy, denies the human being his presumptions of dignity.

Although Morris' universe is nihilistic, his theme impotence, his characters fools and madmen, he renders experience with great richness of detail and evocation, bringing it to life to expose its essential deadness. If his view of reality is limited, it is no more limited than Hemingway's; it is only less simple, less readily appealing. Though in recent years Morris has received a fair amount of critical approbation, he is still undervalued. He may see life through a narrower window than the greatest writers, but he sees its incompleteness distinctively and he sees it whole.

The following listing includes only the novels of the authors discussed in this book.

ROBERT PENN WARREN:
Night Rider. New York: Random House, 1939.
At Heaven's Gate. New York: Harcourt, Brace and Company, 1943.
All the King's Men. New York: Harcourt, Brace and Company, 1946.
World Enough and Time. New York: Random House, 1950.
Band of Angels. New York: Random House, 1955.
The Cave. New York: Random House, 1959.
Wilderness. New York: Random House, 1961.
Flood. New York: Random House, 1964.

SAUL BELLOW:
Dangling Man. New York: Vanguard Press, 1944.
The Victim. New York: Vanguard Press, 1947.
The Adventures of Augie March. New York: The Viking Press, 1953.
Seize the Day. New York: The Viking Press, 1956.
Henderson the Rain King. New York: The Viking Press, 1959.
Herzog. New York: The Viking Press, 1964.

J. D. SALINGER:
The Catcher in the Rye. Boston: Little, Brown and Company, 1951.

RALPH ELLISON:
Invisible Man. New York: Random House, 1953.

FLANNERY O'CONNOR:
Wise Blood. New York: Harcourt, Brace and Company, 1952.
The Violent Bear it Away. New York: Farrar, Straus, and
   Cudahy, 1960.

BERNARD MALAMUD:
The Natural. New York: Harcourt, Brace and Company, 1952.
The Assistant. New York: Farrar, Straus, and Cudahy, 1957.
A New Life. New York: Farrar, Straus, and Cudahy, 1961.

WILLIAM STYRON:
Lie Down in Darkness. Indianapolis: The Bobbs-Merrill Com-
   pany, 1951.
The Long March. New York: Random House, 1952.
Set This House on Fire. New York: Random House, 1960.

EDWARD LEWIS WALLANT:
The Human Season. New York: Harcourt, Brace & World, 1960.
The Pawnbroker. New York: Harcourt, Brace & World, 1961.
The Tenants of Moonbloom. New York: Harcourt, Brace &
   World, 1963.
The Children at the Gate. New York: Harcourt, Brace & World,
   1964.

WRIGHT MORRIS:
My Uncle Dudley. New York: Harcourt, Brace and Company,
   1942.
The Man Who Was There. New York: Charles Scribner's Sons,
   1945.
The Inhabitants. New York: Charles Scribner's Sons, 1946.
The Home Place. New York: Charles Scribner's Sons, 1948.
The World in the Attic. New York: Charles Scribner's Sons,
   1949.
Man and Boy. New York: Alfred A. Knopf, Inc., 1951.
The Works of Love. New York: Alfred A. Knopf, Inc., 1952.
The Deep Sleep. New York: Charles Scribner's Sons, 1953.

The Huge Season. New York: The Viking Press, 1954.

The Field of Vision. New York: Harcourt, Brace and Company, 1956.

Love Among the Cannibals. New York: Harcourt, Brace and Company, 1957.

Ceremony in Lone Tree. New York: Atheneum Publishers, 1960.

What a Way to Go. New York: Atheneum Publishers, 1962.

Cause for Wonder. New York: Atheneum Publishers, 1964.